Proust, Cole Porter, Michelangelo, Marc Almond and me

The National Lesbian and Gay Survey commissions writings by lesbians and gay men on various topics concerned with their lives and lifestyles. *Proust, Cole Porter, Michelangelo, Marc Almond and Me* reflects the diversity of the submissions received from the gay male volunteers and records observations on such themes as their earliest perceptions of homosexuality, and coming to terms with their own sexuality. The diversity lies in the great variety of experiences encountered. While most gay men seem to have a clear idea of their homosexuality from an early age some suffer years of confusion and unsatisfactory marriages in attempting to conform with the perceived norm. Each man's story is unique.

The essays also chart the gay male experience of having to deal with the laws which until the recent past made it a criminal offence for men to have sexual relationships with one another. This led on one level to overt political action; on another level, the result was to form a subculture around public lavatories and other public places – and *Proust, Cole Porter, Michelangelo, Marc Almond and Me* gives frank details of this experience. The book also addresses gay reactions, both negative and positive, to HIV and AIDS, the untimely intervention of which might have decimated the gay male community, but which have succeeded in drawing it together with compassion and a political will.

D1059028

Also available from Routledge

What a Lesbian Looks Like
Writings by Lesbians on their Lives and Lifestyles
from the archives of the National Lesbian and Gay Survey

Walking after Midnight
Gay Men's Life Stories
Hall-Carpenter Archives

Inventing Ourselves
Lesbian Life Stories
Hall-Carpenter Archives

Proust, Cole Porter, Michelangelo, Marc Almond and me

Writings by gay men on their lives and lifestyles from the archives of the

National Lesbian and Gay Survey

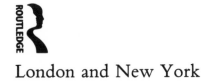

London and New York

First published in 1993 by
Routledge
11 New Fetter Lane, London EC4P 4EE

Simultaneously published in the USA and Canada by
Routledge
29 West 35th Street, New York, NY 10001

© 1993 National Lesbian and Gay Survey

Phototypeset in Linotron Bembo by Intype, London
Printed and bound in Great Britain by
Mackays of Chatham PLC, Chatham, Kent.

British Library Cataloguing in Publication Data
A catalogue record for this book is available from the British Library.

Library of Congress Cataloging in Publication Data
A catalogue record for this book is
available from the Library of Congress.

ISBN 0–415–08914–X

Contents

Foreword

This book is a companion volume to the National Lesbian and Gay Survey's earlier anthology *What a Lesbian Looks Like*. The format is similar, the rules observed in editing the material are the same. However, here all similarity ends. The one factor which unites lesbians and gay men, their attraction to their own gender, is that thing which irrevocably separates them. Although there are meeting points, the lesbian and gay experience is as different as women are from men. Over the years, reading each report that is submitted to NL&GS, it is tempting to make a generalization: a lesbian in coming to terms with her sexuality heads straight for the public libraries while her male counterpart heads straight for the public lavatories. Many women feel that they choose their lesbian sexuality; most men believe they have been gay since birth or early infancy.

Naturally the illegality of sexual acts between men in England and Wales until 1967 – and until later in Scotland and Northern Ireland – and, a quarter of a century later, of acts involving young consenting adults between sixteen and twenty-one years of age colours the male perspective.

The twenty-fifth anniversary of a partially liberating piece of legislation is a time to reflect on the inequalities of existing law. For five years of their adult lives all gay men are supposed to observe a *purdah* not demanded of their heterosexual counterparts. Where the one is deemed mature and responsible enough to make the commitment of a legal marriage at sixteen, and to father children, the other is deemed so immature and irresponsible that he must be protected by legal statute until he is twenty-one. It has been argued that the law exists to protect the young and

vulnerable. As Keith Alcorn has written, 'Young people are vulnerable because of homophobia, not homosexuality.'

Here is the testament of over sixty men, the youngest in his
teens, the eldest in his seventies. There is no political 'right-on-
ness' in the selection. Indeed, there is material here which might
be employed by the lobby opposing reform of the age of consent,
together with material supporting this cause. Gay men have
nothing to hide. Here are the stories of real people whose
emotions have been circumscribed and compromised by law and
who have challenged the unjustness of such legislation with their
lives.

NATIONAL LESBIAN AND GAY SURVEY

During the 1930s a group of academics attempted to record the
feelings and opinions of the person in the street on major issues
of the day. Since then Mass-Observation has undergone many
vicissitudes due largely to funding, or the lack of it, until it was
formalized into a major national project and run from the University of Sussex.

My own involvement with the project began in the early 1980s.
Each submission I made was chased up by a handwritten postcard
from David Pocock, M-O's prime mover at the time, urging me
on. It soon became clear that openly homosexual contributors
were thin on the ground. An idea began to burgeon and, in the
late summer of 1985, I set up the National Lesbian and Gay
Survey in order to redress the balance. Since then lesbian and gay
volunteers nationwide have written and submitted reports on a
wide range of issues pertinent to lesbian and gay life.

The aims of the project are primarily archival, so that
researchers of the future might understand what it was like to
live as a homosexual in the late twentieth century. However, it
became clear that, because the collection is rich in observation
and memory, much of it will be of interest to the reader today.
It was that thought which led to these companion anthologies.

I would first of all like to acknowledge the important part
played by Professor Pocock in the inspiration he provided during
the setting up of the project, and to Dorothy Sheridan who is
continuing his sterling work my thanks for her solidarity. I was
a working volunteer and a director of the Hall-Carpenter Archives
at the time and it was under the auspices of the Archives that

NL&GS operated during its early years. I would like to acknowledge the support and encouragement of Julian Meldrum, the Archives' founder, who first drew me into lesbian and gay archiving, and to the Archives' management team, particularly Peter Daniels, Margot Farnham, Oliver Merrington, David Stewart and Matthew Tagney. Thanks must also go to Kate Wilkinson, my co-director from 1985 to 1988, particularly for her input into the creation of directives.

On behalf of Kerry Sutton-Spence, currently the survey's Women's Director, and myself I would like to acknowledge the encouragement provided by our management group: Steven Barclay, Jerome Farrell, Mandy Hagan, Duncan McDuffie and Rachel Sutton-Spence. An enormous debt of gratitude is owed to Michael Schofield for his financial generosity which has led to our being able to place and maintain a copy of the collection at the Mass-Observation Library at Sussex, together with a further copy available to researchers in Bristol. It is hoped that funds can be raised to provide further copies of the collection for researchers in Scotland, Northern Ireland, North Wales and the North East of England. In the meantime, NL&GS continues its work with quarterly directives to an ever-increasing group of volunteers. This book does not mark the end of a project – it is very much part of the work in progress.

This volume is dedicated to the memory of Raymond Parkes, both a diligent observer and a valued member of our management group.

Kenneth Barrow
Founder, Men's Director

Introduction

NL&GS observers receive a quarterly directive. This is not a questionnaire but rather a series of suggestions of areas the volunteers might care to cover within a given topic. Directives are broad-based and try to approach the subject from every angle. In constructing a directive we are aware that sometimes we are being controversial, sometimes provocative and, occasionally, acting as devil's advocate.

The breadth of directives is matched by the diversity of the views expressed in the observers' written reports. Naturally reports come in which take stances and express opinions quite alien to our own. But no censorship is exercised; everything submitted is logged and placed in the collection. In putting together this anthology we have attempted to reflect this diversity. There are conflicting views, there are contradictions. We make no attempt to draw conclusions; that is the prerogative of the readership whose views will be quite as diverse.

Because we have no control over the structure of the reports or of their content, they do not easily fall into preordained categories. The book is divided into eight parts. Sometimes it may seem that some of the extracts are rather arbitrarily grouped together. However, we have attempted to make the material as assimilable as possible.

All submissions made to NL&GS are entirely anonymous. As a result we are unable to credit any of the extracts to any individual. In order to make them more accessible and to identify serial submissions each author has been allocated a *nom de plume*. Brief biographical details volunteered by each writer can be found in the Index of Authors on p. 194. Observers are instructed to avoid the inclusion of circumstantial details and the naming of individuals. Where such was included in the original report, the circumstantial information has been removed and the names changed. The reason behind this is that there are at least two sides to every story. What might constitute the truth to one might be claimed to be a libel by the other.

Lengthy reports have sometimes been shortened to avoid the unnecessary repetition of common areas of experience. Occasionally, a short section has been isolated because of its particular relevance to the section in which it appears.

NL&GS welcomes all-comers to its volunteer strength. No attempt, other than maintaining gender parity, is made to establish a representative cross-section of the community. Nevertheless, the contributors to this anthology come from a wide variety of backgrounds and lead widely differing lifestyles. The single thing they have in common is that they all identify as gay. Most seemed to have welcomed the opportunity of recording their experiences. Indeed, the contributor you will come to know as Richard, in replying to a directive on long-term relationships, wrote: 'Who needs psychotherapy when we have NL&GS?!'

On behalf of NL&GS I would like to thank not only the authors of the work included in this volume, but all our volunteers for their sheer hard work in making this a vital and worthwhile collection.

Kerry Sutton-Spence
Women's Director

I still hadn't come out to my father. That presented a real problem. . . . One day, as so often happened, out of a complete silence, he looked up from the book he was reading and, *à propos* of nothing, began discussing a point raised by the author as though everyone else in the room was reading the same book. I noticed he was reading Proust.

I cut across what he was saying and said, 'I've got something in common with him.'. . . He asked what that was. I said, 'What do Proust and Auden, Oscar Wilde, Somerset Maugham, Alexander the Great and Tchaikovsky, Michelangelo, Cole Porter, Noël Coward, Housman, John Gielgud and Marc Almond have in common?' He stared at me. 'Add me to the list,' I said. He still stared at me and then he said, 'Who's Marc Almond?'

Simon

1

Beginnings

EDWARD

Homosexuality was a taboo subject in my early childhood and it was around the age of ten when I first heard the word. I remember seeing a news item on the television and I asked my mother what it was all about. She quickly told me that the item was about homos and they were people who prefer members of their own sex. Not knowing that there was such a thing before and not knowing society's views on the subject, I just noted it down with mild interest and went back to what I was doing. I joined the Sea Cadets when I was twelve and it was not long after this that we were sent to Charing Cross for our flag day. Not having been a member long enough to have been given a uniform I had to wear my school uniform, but they did give me a white sailor's hat, a tray of flags and a collecting tin. I soon became bored with the station and Trafalgar Square so I made my way up the Strand, walking by the edge of the pavement and concentrating all my energies on the prospective flag-buying public. People suddenly started to avoid me, refusing to give me money. I didn't understand why until an old lady I had accosted with a shake of my tin said, 'You're not with them are you dear?' I didn't know what she meant but followed her gaze and looked into the road. I then realized that for the last ten minutes I had been part of the 1978 Gay Pride march. I quickly ducked into a shop doorway – I knew what they said about sailors, I'd been ribbed about it often enough at school ever since The Village People brought out 'In the Navy' – and waited for the march to pass. . . .

TOM

I suppose that my first inkling that homosexuality existed was rather nebulous. I can recall my parents and other adults talking about cissies, nancy boys and mother's boys. My early perception of this was a sense that I was like these people.

I remember during the war when I was being evacuated. I was about seven years old. We were on the train from Paddington to Plymouth. The carriage was crowded with civilians and sailors returning to their ships. All the seats were taken and I had to sit on the lap of one of the matelots. I can still feel the sensual pleasure of that contact, smell the serge of his uniform. I often reflect whether this was the reason for my joining the navy later on. . . .

MICHAEL

When I was seven or eight I remember walking around town with my mother looking at and smelling the men. I had a *Blue Peter* annual in which there was a photograph of a football team having a bath; I always wished the water had been clearer or that one of them had been standing up.

Between eight and ten I used to stand in front of a large glass, naked, touching myself. I was becoming aware of – or was I rediscovering? – my body and I got pleasure from doing it, but I did not understand why. I was afraid that I might be discovered, and that my mother would be angry; although I do not remember her saying anything to discourage such behaviour I felt it was wrong. I also got pleasure from exposing myself at my window at night. I did not get any satisfaction from the act itself, but I enjoyed the fear of discovery. I still do the former, though luckily not the latter, but the feeling aroused is different. I no longer fear discovery as no one is likely to come into my room without knocking. I feel that my earlier enjoyment was more innocent. It was a reaction to curiosity, both about my body and other men's, whereas it is now purely for pleasure; and it was not sexual for, although vaguely aware that a man and a woman 'made' a baby, I was not aware of the process. As far as I was concerned my interest in men was natural curiosity, both about the unknown and a desire to know what I would be like when I was older. I had no curiosity about women's bodies because I had frequent baths with my mother and felt I knew all I needed to know about the female form. My father had left when I was two years old and I had therefore never seen a naked man.

There was a school trip to the Pennines when I was ten. We stayed in a youth hostel. I was in a small room with three other boys and the coach driver. I longed to see him undressing and stayed awake until he came into the room, but he turned the light out and I could not see anything. The next day I suffered agonies of disappointment when I heard that the other men who had come on the trip and who were sleeping in a dormitory with the rest of the boys had undressed with the lights still on. I felt ashamed of my wish to see them naked, but I still did not connect it with sexual desires; instead I considered it a phase I would grow out of once I could satisfy my curiosity by looking at my own mature body.

As my body matured I realized that this was not true for I was still interested in men. I do not remember how I became aware of homosexuality, but I know it happened at secondary school. It was considered insulting to call another boy 'gay' or 'bent'. I was frequently called it because I was sensitive and disliked sport and the other boys' rough way of talking and behaving. I may have realized from this that to be gay was to like other men's bodies. This was probably confirmed by facetious remarks made in the shower. I would also have realized that what I had actually had a name. This did not reassure me for I did not want to be something that was treated with antipathy and abuse. Instead, I rejected the idea that I might be gay and consoled myself with the belief that it was only a phase.

I still wanted to believe that it was only curiosity which, once satisfied, would fade. However, I enjoyed looking at other boys in the showers and, far from assuaging my curiosity, it increased it. With this came a new sensation – desire. I began masturbating and I thought of boys not girls. I liked to make myself think of girls but whenever I included them in my fantasies I was always more interested in the boys. I also felt I was violating girls I knew by including them in my fantasies, whereas I did not feel this about boys, they were the same sex and, at the time, I believed that what I imagined could never actually be achieved. It was almost a safety-net, for I thought I was thinking of something I would never actually do. I therefore escaped reality.

This changed when I discovered more about homosexuality. I

realized that men did have sex together and that, rather than escaping reality, I was becoming part of a reality I did not want to accept. I was afraid of being part of a group that was ostracized by the rest of society, for my insecurity demanded that I was accepted by as many people as possible. I was afraid of being an individual and, instead, tried to conform. This led to the creation of a false role, which I deliberately projected, of an ordinary, straight, middle-class boy. This phase lasted from my middle to late teens. The foundation for its destruction was laid by my hubristic concern over the size of my penis. I had one safety rope connecting me to deception and that was the belief (hope?) that I would be revolted by the physical experience if not by the fantasy. This was severed in May 1989. I had discovered the address of our local 'private shop' from pornographic magazines belonging to my stepfather. I consider it highly ironic that, inadvertently, he should have been instrumental in introducing me to my first gay experience and, by that, to myself, for I fear he will be the one least able to understand or accept it – an example of how we are all responsible for what happens to each other even if we do not realize it?

I went to buy something that would enlarge my conceit; instead I was seduced. The man realized I was gay. He told me to come back later. When I returned at the appointed time, after telling the first real lie to my parents, I had enough courage to take off my coat. With hindsight I think I saw a look of pleasure on his face when I did this, but I did not realize the implications at the time. He asked me what I liked, men or women? I was still trying to pretend I liked women and had just a passing interest in men. He asked what I thought of him. I didn't realize what he meant. He asked if I would feel more comfortable with the door locked. Still I did not realize. He asked me what I thought homosexuals did. I answered – still I didn't realize. Then he stepped towards me. I think I at last suspected something for I stepped back. He seemed offended and affronted and asked if I was frightened of him. I replied in the negative, and to show good faith stepped towards him. He grabbed me and gave me my first kiss. We undressed each other. . . .

MERVYN

I remember having what I now know were sexual feelings and fantasies at an early age, even before I started school at five-and-a-half, but I'm not sure. I remember sitting in front of the electric fire in my bedroom supposedly dressing myself in the morning and stuffing my soft toy duck down the front of my trousers to give me a big belly. It gave me what I called a yellow feeling. I also got it when going over a humped-back bridge in the car if it was going fast enough. It was the same feeling that I get when I come. My nanny suddenly came into the room and asked what I was doing with the duck. I was terrified and said, 'Nothing.' It was many years before I recognized these feelings as sexual.

Later, when I was about ten, I used to go and talk to a man who was working on the new houses further down our road. It gave me a thrill, the same old feeling I called yellow. He had an enormous stomach which bulged out above his trousers which were tied round below it with string. I used to think of excuses for talking to him, but he knew they were just excuses and chased me away. I knew I must keep this secret from grown-ups though I had no idea why.

I had one very good friend who was eighteen months younger than me but we spent a lot of time together and frequently I stayed at his house. When I was about thirteen we started masturbating. We never touched one another but did it at the same time, usually before we went to sleep at night, and we talked about it. I said I didn't understand why I thought about men when I did it as, if it was to do with having babies, I would have thought it should have been women I thought about. He was equally puzzled and said that he thought about women with big breasts when he did it. He didn't seem at all shocked by what I'd said.

My family was left-wing and Edward Carpenter was a name well known and talked of in the house but all I knew was that he was a socialist pioneer. I was never allowed to know in what especial way he was so pioneering! I had to wait nearly fifty years till I learned about his sexual politics through the Gay Liberation Front in the 1970s.

It is interesting that being brought up by unchristian adults the moral pressures were very similar to those suffered by children brought up by christians. I thought that I must try to be a good

Communist! It was largely a hangover from the very strong puritan influence on the early Socialists.

My first physical contact with another man consisted of a cuddle and then I think he got my cock out and I came almost immediately. It was an enormous thrill but I was worried. I was afraid someone had seen me go into his house and I knew I couldn't tell the reason. It never occurred to me just to lie that he was just a good friend. I was frightened of his friend who was present. I thought him incredibly ugly. I rather feared they might hold me against my will. They gave me a quite big box of chocolates as I wouldn't stay and this somehow made me more frightened. I took the box and on the way home threw it into an enormous patch of stinging nettles. This was during the war and sweets were rationed and they were very nice chocolates. I knew I had to get rid of them as what could I tell my mother about where I got them? When I got home I went straight into the outside lavatory and wiped my cock and my trousers as I had spilt come on them a bit. I then went upstairs and washed my face. I had been told by a boy at school that grown-ups could tell if you'd come by looking in your eyes. I thought that washing my face would disguise it. I said to myself that I must never do *that* again. In order to avoid meeting the man I changed my route to school so I wouldn't pass his house and in fact did not see him again for two or three years when I ran into him in London. I then leapt on a bus I didn't want to get away. The tragedy is that he was very nice and we could have had a good time and he could have been very supportive to me when I desperately needed it. I tried finding other gays at school, both among pupils and staff, but none would respond to my discreet overtures. They may have been so discreet that they went unrecognized.

The only thing that happened which might be called supportive occurred when I was about fourteen and was a remark by my mother that 'not everyone has to get married . . . some people are happy being everybody's uncle'. This I found to some extent reassuring, though I still thought it my Communist duty to marry and have children and 'be a good citizen'. However, my mother always gave the impression that she would support me whatever.

ANDREW

I was aware of the fact that I was somehow attracted to members of the same sex from a very early age, my earliest remembered memory being when I was four years old and had just started primary school. This guy who was in secondary school would carry my satchel home for me and one day he invited me up to his room while he got changed. I sat on his bed and marvelled at his adolescent body. I realized I was in some way attracted to it though I didn't exactly understand why, as you would expect of a four-year-old.

It wasn't until I was eight that I learned of the word 'homosexual'. I was watching the Comic Strip presentation on Channel Four of *The Famous Five Go Mad in Dorset*, when Uncle Quentin was labelled a homosexual and that it was a crime. I actually thought they were making a joke when they said that, as it felt like the most natural thing in the world to desire and love a member of the same sex. At that time I started imagining pleasure images to help get me off to sleep. A recurring one was that of a tanned, hairless and muscled torso of a man from the neck to the hips.

My first coming-out did not occur until I was fifteen. I was involved with a community play in one of the theatres in Glasgow. It was quite a liberal atmosphere as two other male cast members were out as bisexual. One day I was discussing the film *Torch Song Trilogy* and one of them asked me, 'Are you gay?' I answered 'Yes' and that became the first time that I had admitted not only to others but to myself that I primarily felt both a sexual and emotional bond towards men instead of women. Up until then I had regarded myself as rather non-sexual, neither heterosexual, bisexual nor homosexual, but someone who was born not to find men nor women sexually attractive.

I was actually quite well established on the gay scene in Glasgow and quite well adjusted to my sexuality when I lost my virginity. It was the day of our local switchboard's annual bus run. This guy had been flirting with me all day. I didn't really think that much of it as I assumed he was just being friendly. When we finally got back to Glasgow we went to Austin's Bar. He then went on to make a very obvious pass that even I couldn't have misinterpreted. I was slightly in shock as he was the first man to crack on to me. So I did go off with him. On the corner of Hope Street and West George Street I was kissed in lust for the first time. We hailed a taxi and went back to his place and had the worst sex I have ever had to date.

TONY

My first homosexual encounter was when I was between eight and nine years old with a boy of about the same age who lived a few doors away from us. It was in playing doctors and nurses, only this was doctors and doctors, which I'm sure many of us have played at some time during our younger years. At this age games were of curiosity more than of enjoyment, wondering what another person looked and felt like. At this time I had no idea what a homosexual was, this was purely curiosity, yet I still enjoyed it, and the danger of being caught seemed to make it secret yet enjoyable. The game didn't last very long as the boy moved house shortly after.

I continued through junior school with no real feelings for either sex, and no preference until I was eleven and went into high school. It was about this time that I started to reach puberty and started, not so much to fancy but find some of the lads in my class attractive. It was then I learned about gays and all the images were negative. 'Gays were this and gays were that', and they all hung around toilets and abused young lads, as well as the sick jokes that grew from such myths. My father would occasionally crack jokes about gays and nothing I heard was either a positive view or the truth.

At about thirteen my feelings started slowly getting stronger. I found that I was starting to be aroused by people of the same sex and because of this I started hating myself. I used to lie awake at night, crying myself to sleep, thinking, 'Why God, why me?' At that time I was determined to turn myself straight. I went out with a few girls and tried to make myself believe that I would be happy and my gayness would go away.

At about fifteen I was going out with one of my male school-friend's sisters, and in the summer I used to go camping a lot, mostly in the wilderness of the back garden. Anyway, one night her brother and I decided that we'd camp out together. We lay there chatting and listening to the radio, then he said to me, 'Are you gay?' For a second I wasn't sure what to say. All sorts of things flashed through my mind. What if I admit it, what will they say at school? I didn't want to lose a good friend. In the end I decided to admit it in a joking sense; that way if the worst came to the worst I could say that I was only kidding. 'Of course!' I said, waiting nervously for an answer. 'Then fuck me,' he said. I didn't know what to do. I didn't know if he was testing me or what. I had never been in this situation before and I wasn't just going to climb into his sleeping-bag with him. I still didn't know whether he was testing me or not. So I just unzipped his sleeping-bag and put my hand in. No reaction. He didn't leap out shouting, 'Queer, queer!' I started to feel slightly easier as my hand travelled down his body, then I felt his hand doing the same to me. From that point I relaxed and it went on from there. We made love until about four in the morning, though there was no feeling of love between us. He wouldn't allow me to kiss him, it was purely sexual.

After that there were no feelings of guilt or remorse. To us it was just sex and we enjoyed it. We continued to have sex rarely, only about once every six months, and that was all it was. I didn't have any desire for a relationship, but I did wish he would let me kiss him. During my last few years at school I had three other similar experiences, again just sex, no love, and at the time it didn't matter. For a few years after I left school I still couldn't fully accept my feelings because of the prejudice and ignorance of society as a whole, and I still thought I could change my feelings. When I started work at the supermarket there was a girl who used to hang around the store a lot and I got chatting to her. Eventually, confused, I asked her to go out with me. At the time I wanted to love a woman or at least to know if I *could* love a woman. A few months later I was at home watching television and I saw and video-taped a film about gay teenagers. Watching the film I could see myself in it, everything that had happened to him was happening to me. The main character even had the same name as me. At the end I sat and cried for half-an-hour, it moved me so much. It was then that I knew what I must do and I finally came to terms with myself.

I finished with my girlfriend and decided that I couldn't handle this alone, that I needed to talk to someone. I had already 'brain-picked' my best friend without him knowing and dropped into conversation 'What if I was gay?' to which his reply was, 'Well, that's another girl for me!' From that answer I knew that if I could trust anyone I could trust him. So I sat him down and gave him a brief sealed letter saying, 'Please watch the tape that's on the video. I hope this will explain why I have been acting so weird lately, and I'll be in the car when you've finished watching it. P.S. Note, even the same name as myself.' So he watched the film and then got into the car and said, 'Well, do you want to talk about it?' I couldn't speak, I was so nervous. My mouth was moving but no words were coming out. We drove for about an hour. I was trying to think of something to say but I couldn't. Eventually we got back to my house and he said, 'Well?' I don't know how, but the words finally came out and we talked for hours. At last I wasn't alone.

GREG

My first realization of the existence of homosexuality must have been through playground taunting with me on the receiving end, so I'd say that by the time I was seven I knew what they meant when I was accused of being a poof. I also knew what a real poof was like. I have very vivid memories of spending an occasional evening in the West End as a child after a day's shopping with my parents and being totally fascinated by the hordes of very attractive, very well-dressed young men walking around the streets together. I was clever enough to realize just what was going on and I knew that that was what I wanted to do one day. It was a very positive image. I also remember both my parents constantly moaning at me, telling me to stop staring at all the men. I was very positive as a child and thought nothing of taking on the role of a fairy in a pink tutu in a school play when no one else would for some strange reason!

I would often fall madly in love with the exceptionally beautiful fellow male students. My sister who is gay recalled when I came out, 'I can remember you ranting on about how beautiful so-and-so's skin was when you were only five years old.' I thought nothing of sending anonymous Christmas and birthday cards, hand-made of course, to the one I thought was the most beautiful male in the school at the time. I always felt very positive about being attracted to other boys and about wanting to become part of what I'd seen in London. I didn't realize that this made me the poof everyone kept telling me I was, the two just didn't seem to connect. When I did connect the two I decided to act straight and ignore my feelings which was a really stupid move as the whole community where I lived had already placed a large pink label on me.

My first physical gay experience was snogging my older cousin when I was about fourteen under the pretence of practising kissing for his girlfriend (wasn't she the lucky one?). This wasn't either good or bad. At the time I felt nothing other than curiosity as to what the lump rising in his trousers looked like. I didn't get to find out. I'd just turned nineteen when I actually slept with a man for the first time. This was not a good experience. He was supposed to be my therapist but he took it one step too far by seducing me. He was about forty, not very attractive and not very caring. I still feel ill thinking about it. I spent a long time in great doubt and slept with two women and a straight guy, all of whom failed to inspire me. Then I turned twenty-one and decided to go and find what I was looking for.

KEVIN

I first identified homosexual feelings when I was about ten. I was able to get an orgasm by then, though there was no ejaculation for a couple of years. I know that I female-identified at this time. I achieved orgasm not by conventional jerking off but by putting my penis between my legs and manipulating it with my legs. It was when I was ten that I had my first relationship with another boy. He was my cousin and was about eighteen months older than me. I suspect it was his idea rather than mine. Our sex involved role playing (yes, it was doctors and nurses, and I was always the nurse), kissing, and a simulation of the missionary position. This went on for about six months, though it may have been less. I recall sometime later he was interested in a girl in the neighbourhood. I remember saying within the earshot of several other boys that he had practised kissing on me. He didn't speak to me for months. Later I introduced him to the only girl I ever fancied. They just celebrated their silver wedding. For years it was his looks against which all other men were judged.

I female-identified in lots of games in adolescence. In the gangs I was with, where there was any physical sexual exchange, I always dressed up, for example, as the woman who judged the lengths of the others' cocks. This may have been because genitally I developed late, but I think there was always a feeling of 'difference'. But I didn't have another relationship of more than a few minutes duration for about nine years. Even then I female-identified. The relationship was with a married man and I became his other woman! It was a few years before I sorted this out. I think the old images of homosexual stereotyping were to do with this female identification. Certainly in the early days of gay liberation in England femininity in men found permission. I never lisped or minced around but I dressed in a way that flouted male stereotypes, masses of chiffon scarves and so on.

My first sexual experiences were all happy. I really loved my cousin. We knew we had to keep our activities secret because anything between the legs was lavatorial to our families and thus to be ashamed of. But our ecstasy was certainly heightened by rebelling against our parents in this way. My middle to late adolescence, and a little beyond, gave me expression only through public lavatory contact – mainly 'under the wall'. It was all I had. I lived in the remote countryside and had only small towns for contact. I have today a terrible abhorrence for cottage sex.* Since then I have learned avenues that are pleasanter. But then it was all I had. And I have to admit it was in a cottage that I met the great love of my life.

The only person I knew to be gay apart from the one or two people I identified from under the wall encounters, neither of whom I ever spoke to outside, was a schoolfellow in the year ahead of me. I had unwittingly once got him into trouble for an unrelated incident so he never spoke to me and we never shared our homosexuality. We never had sex together. I think we were once rivals for someone we both fancied. Neither of us, as I recall, scored with him. I see this schoolfellow around in London from time to time and we have a brief chat, thirty years too late. When I went away to college I continued to have under the wall encounters which led to a quick bedroom scene or sex in the bushes or the cemetery or other such delightful venues. This led sometimes to conversation and I began to work out who I was. I always say I came out before it was invented. That was in 1963, three months after I started college, that I came out to my mother. Nearly a quarter of a century later she is just beginning to come to terms with it. There was a lot of tears and anguish. At this remove I can't quite recall whether it was she who suggested I go to see a psychiatrist or whether it seemed the only thing I

---

* Cottage = public lavatory. Hence 'cottage sex', 'cottaging'.

could reasonably do. I found one through my GP at college and went for 'the cure'. This consisted of various methods of aversion therapy. I was given a square wooden box with a wire from it and a kind of press-studded bandage which you attached to your wrist. There was a bell-push on the box. At high points during masturbation you were supposed to press the bell-push and you got a slight electric shock in the wrist. It was, even at a practical level, quite the most ridiculous operation. One didn't seem to have enough hands! And it didn't seem to have much effect except that one had rather more masochistic fantasies, thus utilizing the pain! The next stage was the use of an emetic. This was chemical. You were given an injection which facilitated sexual fantasy and made you vomit at the same time. Fortunately, before this was tried on me, the psychiatrist asked if I really wanted to be cured. To my relief I heard myself saying 'No' and he told me to stop wasting his time. I realize now that all I had wanted in going to him was someone to talk to about my homosexuality. In those days before decriminalization, homosexuality was generally perceived as a problem, as a curse everyone would want to have removed. How many young men and women must have gone through with that sickening and degrading process? I remember writing in my diary or somewhere, 'Will I be able to write poetry or cry at sad movies afterwards?' I didn't want my personality changed. He was only interested in taking something away from me. Putting something in its place had nothing to do with the therapy. Anyway, the realization that this wasn't for me finally sorted me out. The times they were a-changing anyway, but not fast enough. A couple of years later I was involved in a court case and it hit the national press and I was forced OUT in a big way! Je ne regrette rien. I've never looked back.

ROGER

I was born in a small town in south Buckinghamshire, into a rural working-class family where values and lifestyle were basically conservative. I can seriously never remember homosexuality being mentioned at home, but I suppose I became aware of its existence through playground taunts – 'poofter' and so on, though not necessarily directed at myself. However, I certainly remember feeling different from many other kids even at primary-school level. I simply wasn't interested in sports of any kind – give me the Wendy house any time! I remember dressing up in Mum's old clothes and trying on make-up, not in itself any evidence of homosexuality but it is surprising to me just how many gay blokes have been through that type of experience. I particularly remember another kid at primary school who used to bring dresses to school to camp around in. Needless to say, he ended up a drag queen! Nearly all my friends at primary school were girls and again this seems to be common among many gay men.

I certainly had feelings about my own inclinations well before I ascribed any label to them. I can remember going to secondary school and experiencing quite strong realizations that I was attracted to other boys. I went to a single-sex boys' grammar school. I hate to disappoint you but if anything *did* go on there, I wasn't included! No doubt the rugby squad were all wanking each other off behind the bike-sheds, but I wasn't part of it. Actually I was sexually very naive and a bit of a late starter I suppose. I can recall someone asking me about wanking at the age of twelve. I'd never actually heard the term before, although I was certainly doing it! It was always over other boys as well. I didn't perceive my picture of Donny Osmond on the wall as being at all sexual, but who knows? Certainly I was not interested in looking at the porno magazines which the other boys brought into school, in fact I found them utterly revolting, and as a result was called a queer. That didn't really bother me and it didn't particularly stick as a term of abuse, but certainly I wasn't a 'lad' in either appearance or behaviour.

The images of homosexuality I first remember were on the television and were invariably camp. Let's see: there were the gay couple in the Hylda Baker programme about the pub, one very tall and mute, the other small and effeminate, and Hylda used to say, 'And what are *you* today, Gilbert?' to the tall one and, after a twirl, it was, 'Oh, you're one of *those*, are you?' Then there was Larry Grayson, John Inman, of course ('I'm free!'), and Dick Emery's gay character, Honky-tonk. Not exactly positive images, but they all make me laugh even now. There goes my political credibility. I certainly never felt the inbuilt animosity towards homosexuality which others seemed to display. I remember a school debate where I simply could not understand why people were opposed to people being gay. By then I was politicized, although in a somewhat reactive and oppositional way. Having made it to grammar school, I was a staunch Tory at the age of twelve, but by fourteen I was in the Anti-Nazi League and involved in the Young Socialists. It was then that I read about gay rights and felt an innate empathy, not one which I realized at the time was anything to do with what *I* was, in fact I find that impossible to work out, exactly when I decided that I was gay. Maybe there wasn't a definite moment of decision, it was more something I became aware of as time went on.

I was 'out' to a lot of people before I had sex with anyone. Certainly I was supportive of gay rights in a political context and spoke out on behalf of gays and no doubt some people did think 'Eh?', but I would have absolutely died if I would have thought anyone would have guessed. Strange how my own perception can be so positive on a political level but so very opposite in personal terms. I went to a further education college to do two A-levels and buried myself in a variety of activities – politics, hospital radio – and I was at that time psychologically repressing myself in not making any attempt to appear attractive. On going to university I remember going to the Societies Fayre and talking to a woman who happily told me she was going to join the Gaysoc. Even though I would have loved to join there was no way I would have done that at that stage. Rather than coming out at university I ended up getting deeply involved in evangelical Christianity. This was another sign of my own hiding and self-repression. The first person I ever told about myself was, at that time, my best friend at university who was in the Christian Union and on whom I had an incredible crush. At that time I didn't want to be gay and within that context it was quite a supportive friendship. My parents were told when I was twenty-two, although Mum said she had known for a long time. It wasn't exactly ideal, it all came in the middle of a tremendous row. I had been unemployed for over a year after giving up a very high-pressured job in advertising in London at about the same time as I gave up evangelical Christianity and started to come to terms with myself and my sexuality. All this had left me pretty incapable of doing anything and my continued unemployment added to pressures at home. I can't say Mum was exactly delighted about it all, but over the years she has become a lot more accepting. Dad simply doesn't talk about it (do dads talk?) but really I can't complain, they've very supportive of me as an individual and part of that is my own sexuality.

TIM

When I was at junior school I can remember walking to school one day feeling quite depressed and thinking, 'Why can't I be a girl? Wouldn't it be fantastic if everything just stopped and I could be transformed into a little girl instead of a little boy?' I used to love dressing up in my older sister's and mother's clothes. I don't know why. I've often thought that maybe I felt my sister got better treatment from my parents because she was a girl so, subconsciously, I felt that if I was a girl I'd be treated better.

I can remember funny experiences of going into toilets when I was thirteen or fourteen, having long staring sessions at older men and wanking myself off at the urinals. I think I properly realized about homosexuality about a year later when I met a boy round at someone's house that I frequented a lot down the street. He was gay and he had a friend at high school who was gay. I realized I was gay too although different from these two people in personality and such. I went out with one of them but it didn't really last very long. I once went to meet him for dinner. We went down a passage behind some shops, talked and kissed. The thought of this still puts a glow in my stomach. He was plump, quite camp and effeminate. He took me to a club that was supposed to be gay but turned out to be mixed. We sat in this alcove holding hands and kissing. It was early and there were not many people in the club. A straight couple came to sit near, but saw us and walked off, the girl looking quite disgusted but unable to say anything. We finished seeing each other but I remember feeling brilliant, and happy defining myself as gay.

PETER

As a child, before school even, I had mental visions of naked men, though not very clearly delineated. I imagined several policemen kneeling around and using an enormous chamber pot. I also made up stories as I still do before going to sleep, stories of me and men, not in sexual contact as I knew nothing of that then, of course, but being comforted by them. This was stimulated by the large number of films I saw as a child. The list of my loves is a potted history of male film actors: Ramon Novarro and Gary Cooper and, at the age of fifteen, Tyrone Power. I kept most of this to myself, though I wrote to Gary Cooper about a dream I'd had of him and got a non-committal reply.

Kissing and sex were for a long time separated. I would have loved to kiss some men. Two, at separate times, were men we knew as visitors to the family, and they were the objects of real love. But it was all pure and, though my family teased me about my 'pashes' as they called them, they did not seem then, or later, to see this as a manifestation of anything.

On one occasion when I was aged about six I was asked by one of the crew of a pleasure boat we were on what I was going to be when I grew up. 'A bachelor,' was my reply. Later, I had two dreads about the future: one was going to war and the other was marriage. Why was I certain about being a bachelor and why full of dread about marriage? Was it merely prophetic wishful thinking? I did not have to experience either of these fears.

My first sexual encounter was at boarding school when I was nine or ten. A boy two or three years older than me showed me his erect penis and we spent the rest of the evening fondling each other's. It was a very happy experience. I realized that this was what it was all for. As I remember, however, we did not kiss nor did I think of my film actors. In *A Taste of Honey* Helen says to Jo that, though you can enjoy the second, the third and even the fourth time, there's no time like the first. 'It's always there.' This is a very perceptive statement and, though I did not later yearn for him at all and I did not see him again after I left school, I shall always regard that experience as a blessing, eclipsed only by my first encounters with my partner sixteen years later. I certainly did not feel guilty. I have since learnt that, after a very happy marriage, he is now dead.

Later I did feel guilty about masturbation which, apparently, was sinful. I had a strong, narrow Christian upbringing. However, I read of friendships between men, close, loving, but without sex. There were plenty of novels about such relationships especially school stories, and I fantasized about some of my male teachers. I read these books now, full of unspoken subtexts which can only point to latent homosexuality in the characters and authors.

At my three schools there was only that one encounter. At my secondary boarding school it was totally absent, despite all the boys in my house showering together and I, as a fag, seeing my prefects in their unashamed and splendid nakedness in their study while I made their tea. I fell in love, secretly but not seriously, with a few other boys. Sex and love were still separate.

My brother, a few years older, may have been gay. He was killed in the war but no evidence of love for anyone was apparent.

Once when I was fourteen I tried to explain to a twenty-five-year-old man that I loved him. He was very gentle and puzzled about it. We never referred to it after that evening and when he was killed in the war I wrote in my diary that 'he carried my guilty secret to the grave'. When I was about twenty I told a married teacher colleague that I was in love with him. I had seen him showering and he was very beautiful. He told me kindly that I was probably not homosexual really if no buggery had ever taken place; mutual masturbation was not really a sign of anything definite. How wrong could he be?

I still felt guilty. One man who picked me up – I was seventeen, he was ten years older than me – told me how wrong this feeling was. If we enjoy it, why not do it? I did not talk to him at length but what he said must have affected me, so I went on. I lived in a town of twenty thousand people in New Zealand. My visits to cottages when I was fifteen must have been reported and a policeman made me walk in front of him to my mother's shop and tell her. He was kind enough not to charge or arrest me but my mother was deeply, deeply distressed and wanted to know why I did it. There was and is no answer to that question despite glib assurances from people who have never been homosexual. A child of five who has visions of men's penises and asks, as I did once, 'When will I have a big one?' is hardly 'going through a stage'. But I did not tell my mother this. Later, when I had my first love affair, she was incredulous and sad, but relieved that I was not going to live with him when I went to university after the war. She died a year or so later aged only sixty-two. But she had had an exhausting life, having been widowed in 1933 and brought up three children on a shopkeeper's income. Was it this that hastened her death, or my homosexuality, my brother's death in Egypt or my sister's unsatisfactory marriage?

I no longer felt guilty about the large number of partners I had nor of my cottaging but I was not sure if being homosexual was wholly acceptable. I had read little about it. One day in the university library, I searched the catalogue and came upon Edward Carpenter's *The Intermediate Sex*. Many years earlier, while still at school, I had found Leslie Weatherhead's *The Mastery of Sex* in a friend's library. I read only the piece on masturbation not the piece on 'Inversion, or Homosexuality'. Both of these topics were in the chapter 'The Mishandled Sexlife'. Carpenter, however, was a great help and seemed to suggest that it was quite common and that not all of us were to be found in cottages, which is where I found most of my partners.

So I came to terms with it and secretly enjoyed myself. There were plenty of attractive men to be found, especially when I left my home town and went to the large city where the university was. Despite one or two bizarre episodes I was unharmed and not found out. I only wanted a permanent lover when I would probably become less promiscuous.

In 1948 I met my present partner who was on a visit to my home town, more or less picking him up at night at a piecart, not a cottage, in the centre where I had gone after a film to find some sex. It changed our lives totally, but before I was prepared to make the change I needed yet more confirmation. I spent an afternoon in the Auckland Reference Library with Havelock Ellis's volume on inversion in *The Psychology of Sex*. All was well, I realized, as the librarian locked it back in the glass case. A longtime friend to whom I came out confirmed this. And so, without guilt, without shame and with a certain sense of warm satisfaction and hope, we set out on our long journey together.

MAURICE

I went into a boys-only boarding-school from the age of five years until seventeen. The school was a school for boys who were the sons of officers in the army regulars. Also it was a school for boy choristers for the south of England cathedral in the grounds of which it was situated. We only had six weeks in the whole year away from the school. During term time we were not allowed out at all.

It would be best to say that I was well aware of homosexuals and the active part of it from the age of fourteen years. This was because the older boys would come into our beds at night. When it first happened to me I liked all of what we did, but I would not let anyone penetrate me; anything else, but I made a stand against that. I think I thought it was a positive thing so far as I was concerned and I looked forward to the nights when a certain older boy came to my bed. He was something different to me.

It was not a question that I loved him but more that he always showed concern and was kind to me.

My first real experience, which was to last over a year or so, was when I first met a boy the same age as myself, seventeen-and-a-half years of age, when we both signed up for the army. The whole day we spent together, and the evening. In that day we got so attached to each other that as soon as we knew the date we had to go into the army we spent the whole week together at my home. We slept together and had full sex morning and night. We were both well aware of what we were doing and never had any regrets at all, in fact quite the reverse. As luck would have it we stayed together about two years, but he was killed in Rangoon in the Burma War. I got to the hospital which the army had taken over a few minutes before he died. There were tears in my eyes. I brushed them aside by saying, 'It's effing hot in here', and wiped my face as though I was wiping off sweat! But I loved that chap more than I have ever loved anyone since.

CHARLES

At the age of fourteen I discovered that I got an erection when seeing fellow pupils undressing for the gymnasium or swimming baths and the sight of genitals gave me a feeling of excitement. I found that, on actual physical contact with another boy, either during play or while sharing an activity in physical exercises, I perceived a tingling sensation and an urge to stroke and touch. I know it is not uncommon for feelings of this nature to be aroused during simple horseplay or a friendly wrestling game, but I found that sight and touch of a fellow pupil or schoolfriend in shorts or a bathing costume sent a tremor through my body, and I got the inevitable erection. Later on in my schooldays I had a special friend who shared the same excitement as I did on mutual touching and fondling of each other's genitals and we eventually indulged in wanking each other.

I mixed with both girls and boys during my leisure hours and, in fact, tried to date girls which was the 'normal' thing to do, but I found, at this early age, that petting with girls did not stir any feeling, nor did I get that tingling which was felt when in the company of boys. In my early days in the 1930s there were no books or magazines published for the homosexual male. There were plenty of what are now called 'soft' and the odd 'hard' porn girlie magazine and where prominence was given to the female model, scantily clad or full frontal, this did not stir any feeling in me whatsoever. If, however, I saw a girlie magazine showing a picture of a man and woman together in some intimate pose, my attention was immediately drawn to the figure of the male and it was on his form that I directed all my attention and feeling. I remember even fantasizing that I was the partner in the pose and I would imagine that he was fondling me and I would ache for the chance to touch his penis.

I am able to go back in time in my memory a half century when homosexuality was looked upon either as a plague of the mind or the practice of a male who had been spawned by the Devil no less. Getting out of the closet in my earlier days was a formidable proposition as one was automatically earmarked for disinheritance from the family, loss of one's job and being the target for alienation by 'normal' people, and even being referred to a mental institution.

Despite the outside world being fraught with all these and more perilous obstacles I actually came out in the mid-1940s at the age of twenty. My decision to make known my sexuality was, I suppose, taken after having been seen constantly in the company of young men and showing no interest whatsoever in girls, which was demonstrated quite clearly when I declined invitations to mixed parties and could not resist ogling the boys when I was in mixed company. During social get-togethers with male friends, where perhaps a friendly wrestling match would take place, I would feel myself drawn towards whoever I was playing with and get an erection. It became apparent to my friends that I was 'queer'. After a weekend with a close friend during which I slept with him, fondled him then kissed him and tried to penetrate him, which he firmly resisted, he told my parents of my advances. I was home on leave from the army and, as any such activity was a serious criminal offence in those days in civil life and most gravely dealt with in the services, I had to face the consequences of my actions somehow. Upon being questioned by both my parents and those of my friend, I cannot even to this day explain how I found the courage to explain that I was sexually orientated towards other men. I well remember the rage of my father and the subsequent tirade of abuse I received plus the threats to expose me to the army command. This latter caused me the greater concern as I was aware that I would not only lose my rank and identity but be publicly disgraced. I reluctantly agreed to visit a family doctor in the company of my parents. The thought of finding myself committed to an institution paralysed me with fear. I broke down and promised to 'mend my ways' and act like a man and be 'normal'. I resisted any urge to seek the company of other men and became a loner.

It was during this self-imposed interlude of keeping myself to myself, when I devoted all my efforts into training and proving myself as a model soldier, that I was promoted to platoon sergeant in charge of thirty men and posted overseas. I had previously suffered unbearable tortures when living in accommodation shared by twenty or thirty men, sleeping so close together, bathing and with ablutions in a naked state each day. I was permanently uptight, wrestling with the problem of keeping myself forcibly celibate. In my new capacity I had access to intimate relationships with my men insofar as to winning their confidence and support as well as them, in turn, being subservient to me. Eventually, however, the stifled sexual desire within me resurfaced and, in defiance of the military code of conduct, I was able to select one of my platoon who had shown tendencies towards me that hinted he was infatuated by me. I exploited this and was soon in a position to take him as my lover, both knowing full well that we must keep our relationship strictly private. Had he ever disclosed what we got up to he was aware that his word would be worthless against my rank and authority, so it was to his peril to do so. To have been able to practise my homosexuality albeit dangerously while serving in the forces was, in retrospect I suppose, some kind of achievement. On reading about the current campaign to revise the armed services ruling on the regulations regarding homosexuality I can endorse the view that one's sexual orientation need not necessarily impair one's efficiency in carrying out one's duties if one can separate the two, as has equally been proven in other professions.

My younger brother was 'initiated' when, on one of my home leaves, I shared a bed with him. He was just sixteen years old at the time but he was a very well formed boy. On our first night together I played around with him and he responded without much tuition. We made love a number of times and for several years after that. Eventually he also declared himself a homosexual.

He never faced my parents with his 'secret' but carried on with his affairs unknown to them. I left home, and for some twenty years my parents and I never met.

SAM

By the age of twelve or thirteen I knew I was 'different'. I was involved in mutual masturbation both at the school gym club and in class. I remember clearly the talk of the Wolfenden Report and all the talk of queers at the time. Certainly I did not understand my feelings at first. I knew that I enjoyed the company of men more than that of women, and I found some men sexually attractive. I did not, however, know what this was and thought that I was just growing up and going through a phase. As the object of my admiration and desires was a local sporting hero no one seemed to appreciate what I was going through.

Following my move from home to London and then into National Service I was in an all-male environment and I soon realized there were other guys about who were homosexual. At first I could not understand how they could be so open about their sexuality and later I wondered why they seemed to want everyone to know they were gay. As time went by I got to know them and from this to understand and admire them. Having said that, I guess that I was twenty-one or two before I actually accepted my sexuality and it was another five or six years before I was happy about it. In this case being happy equated to being positive.

My first gay experience was when I was about twenty. The physical side was fine but it was a hole-in-the-corner event as gays were not exactly welcome in the RAF. (After twenty-four years in the service I can say nothing has changed.) I soon realized that the only way to be happy in physical encounters was to arrange them so that they took place in private and when off base for weekends, etc. The relief of knowing that no one might come in made for a far happier approach to sex and my gayness in general.

OLIVER

There was a curious game I played around the age of nine to ten, both in my last years at primary school and when I arrived at prep school. This involved the idea of 'kissy-itis', a 'disease' of, I think, my own invention which caused me to go around kissing everyone in the playground. At primary school I vaguely remember having some accomplices. The 'disease' was, of course, passed on by kissing, so everyone kissed had to behave similarly. On the first occasion I tried the game at prep school, another boy 'sneaked' on me to the teacher in charge, and I remember being told off very severely. Once I had gone on from prep school to main school at the age of eleven I had gained a little knowledge of names for homosexuals as part of the ordinary schoolboy vocabulary of abuse, but almost none of this language meant anything to me at all. Thereafter I began to play with myself under the bedclothes after lights-out, and very occasionally saw the pictures in girlie magazines the other boys sometimes got hold of, but until the age of fourteen or fifteen I could say that my sex life, and my level of interest in it, were virtually nil.

My first physical sexual experience of any kind with another person was with my brother who is four years older than me. We shared a bed when staying at Grandma's for half-term, and one morning he reached over and started wanking me. I did the same for him and we both came. This, in itself, was almost a new experience for me. My experiments in the bath had involved orgasm, but I never produced any liquid. I think I remember it as an unpleasant occasion, mainly because it felt very furtive and naughty. We had several similar experiences during subsequent holidays, and I rather think I disliked the experience increasingly on each occasion. I may even have asked him to stop. In any case, after a while it did stop. There was no question of coercion. The sex came about simply as a result of his hesitantly initiating it and my not putting up any resistance or objections. I think I was about fifteen when all this took place.

During the same year I began in the timidest possible way to experiment with sex with other people. After lights-out in the dormitory I began to play some sort of game with the boy in the next bed. It was an all-boys school and I was a boarder. I can't remember exactly how the game began but it did involve placing my hand on his bedclothes. I think there was some element of reciprocation – perhaps it was some sort of dare whereby we took turns to go further and further. In any case it led eventually to my putting my hand inside his bedclothes, reaching further and further down the front of his pyjamas until

I eventually touched his cock. I think he got as far with me as well. I do remember that he showed quite a bit of reluctance at various stages. Presumably he was less interested in the game than I was or, at least, more paranoid about discovery. The whole game took place in total silence, or with the quietest of whispers. I seem to remember that, on one occasion, he came as soon as I had started wanking him. This was the only time throughout the game that either of us came. It must have gone on, intermittently, for several months with the other boy becoming more and more reluctant to take part until eventually I asked him if he wanted it to continue. He whispered, 'No.' However, at the beginning of each term one was quite likely to be landed with different neighbours, and I tried something the same with the next boy to move into an adjacent bed only, this time, for some reason, the game never involved him, only me 'seeing how far I could go' without him noticing. Indeed I am pretty sure he was asleep every time I did this. In any case I never got further than just touching his cock. I tried this second version of the game on my next neighbour as well. However, on one night he was awake and indicated that he was aware of something before my hand had got under the bedclothes. For some reason I tried again later that night, and this time I had just about got my hand inside when he grabbed it! He then told me he wanted nothing of whatever it was I was doing, and that put a stop to me doing anything sexual with another boy for the rest of my time at school. Looking back I am amazed that I dared to do what I did. There were over twenty boys in the dormitory, and the beds were very close together.

I took a year out between school and university during which time I kept up a voluminous correspondence with Antony, my best schoolfriend, who is nearly a year older than me. As my sixth form went by I had become increasingly worried about my being turned on by my own sex. I developed a little bit of a crush on another boy in my year, though all I could imagine was embracing him in a manly sort of way, and even fantasized about making advances to some of the resident masters who were rumoured to be 'queer' and found it a great source of comfort that I could be friends with Antony without there being anything sexual between us. We discussed all sorts of issues in our letters, including sex in a fairly abstract way. In the summer of my year off I went to stay with him for a few days and it was during one of the long walks we were always going off on that we each revealed to the other that we thought we were gay! I suspect that for Antony there was a little more to it, even that he had a slight crush on me but, since at this time I professed myself entirely unable to understand what love was in any form, I wasn't emotionally involved at all. Anyway, the next morning I got into bed with him, the first time I had ever been naked in bed with anybody, and the touch of another person's flesh against me all over was unforgettably arousing, even though Antony's body has never particularly attracted me. We sucked each other off, I think, and since I was to depart later that day, that was that. I remember feeling very tongue-tied and unhappy for the rest of that morning. I felt very much that the nature of our relationship had changed irrevocably and that we would never be able to talk as freely with each other again.

I wasn't returning home immediately but was off to Yorkshire for a Young MENSA weekend, a short residential holiday. It was while on the train that I started what has ever since been an obsessive pastime when on long journeys alone: pretending to be asleep I allow myself to come into contact with any reasonably good-looking man sitting next to me or opposite me. Nothing has ever come of this, and I have only very rarely got the impression that my contact was actively returned, but it certainly passes the time.

Anyway, having stayed awake all night watching videos and having discussions with various groups of people, I eventually wound up in the early morning with only one boy of about my own age for company. We went for a walk around dawn, and on returning to the holiday building we collapsed in a room full of crashed-out people. While the other boy apparently dropped off I rested my body against his and gradually eased my hand into his trousers. When I reached the point of having his cock out and fondling it he suddenly woke up, jerked away, did up his trousers and dashed out of the room. I remember feeling rather devil-may-care about this, sort of 'well, if he's screwed up about it, sod him.' And that was the end of that. Just before starting life at university I invited Antony to stay with me for a few days. I was alone in my parents' flat and we had my parents' double-bed to ourselves. Of course we had sex every night, on the whole enjoyably, but most of the holiday was pervaded by the same feelings of awkwardness and inarticulacy that had appeared after our first sexual encounter. However, of all the people I knew until the time I admitted to myself that I was gay, his friendship was invaluable in discussing and coming to terms with my sexuality.

RON

I first became aware of homosexuality after reading about the Lord Montagu case in the national newspapers in 1954. My first loving feelings towards other members of my own sex were at school at the age of six in 1939 just before the war when a fourteen-year-old cousin of my late mother's, Joey, visited the house. He looked so handsome to me, and I told him I loved him. How I plucked up the courage at that tender age I will never know.

I learnt about sex at school in 1946. The boys were always indecently assaulting me. I didn't see it as homosexuality, but something we weren't supposed to be doing, but I got great pleasure from when they masturbated me. Of course, being constantly indecently assaulted by a gang of boys at school was to arouse my first physical expression of my homosexuality. It wasn't a happy experience at the time because it was quite frightening, a gang of bigger, older boys bundling me into a toilet and undoing my braces and taking my trousers and underpants down and getting another boy to keep rubbing my cock in short frantic bursts. I knew I had to get what I called a 'rude' feeling in my cock, but I couldn't concentrate with some of the other boys repeatedly shouting out, 'Come on Jones!' It was on the insistence of the ringleader that the boy ruthlessly rubbed my cock until it seemed he had been doing it for all eternity. I thought it would go on forever. In the end I decided I would give them the happy ending they wanted. My mind now fully attuned to the rubbing of his fingers I finally capitulated and submitted to him and all of them. I felt really happy about it when later I did it in private with other boys at the school and afterwards, when I consider what an erotic way to be introduced to sex it was for me personally.

LESTER

I was brought up in council care from the age of one day to sixteen years old. I was aware of being very distrustful of people, men more than women, and my first sexual experiences were based on lust rather than love. I became aware of being gay around age eleven. I met someone in boarding school who I loved but he was bisexual and I was never sure that he returned my emotional feelings and, being rather shy, I rarely asked him as he was also someone who used to beat me up so that others didn't think he was a queer. I did try to explain to my stepfather that I liked boys more than girls when I was sixteen but he said all boys go through it. I was referred to the Albany Trust but I didn't get any help. Then I was told by the council psychiatrist to go to a clinic. This was a confusing time as the people at the clinic told me I could be 'cured', so although I didn't worry about being gay I felt isolated and alien. Part of the problem was that I had been raped at the age of eight-and-a-half by three older boys who left me literally bruised all over. Then when I was thirteen an older man took me from boarding school and kept me for two days in a bedroom. On both occasions I didn't have any pleasant feelings because I was used for their satisfaction. So I would have to say that my image of gays is mixed. I am aware of loathing for myself and hatred for men who molest children.

After reaching twenty-one years of age and still attending the clinic I was told by my child-care officer that gay was a state not a medical illness which came as a bit of a shock, also I was very angry at the deceit of others who knew this and had just let me go on thinking I was being cured. The first person to be helpful was a black guy two years older who became my partner in a relationship and he was very patient. He needed to be too. I have never been very extrovert so it was something I hadn't dared to talk about to too many people. The teachers in the council board-ing schools were mainly ignorant and to discuss being gay would mean everyone would know and they would mark your case-notes with it. It was treated as a plague or dreadful disease. My child-care officer and his wife were very helpful and supportive and their home was the only place for a long time that I felt part of. It was through them that I started reading seriously at the age of sixteen, Jean Paul Sartre, Jean Genet, Kafka, Proust, and started discovering an unknown world or, rather, a dimension of the world. It was then I started my own education and started along the road of socialism. All the places I had lived in up to twenty-one were run by or were controlled by the local council so being gay and left-wing were something to hide. It also showed me the totalitarian, fascistic atmosphere in these 'homes'. As I have said it was a very confusing time and I felt very lonely, alien and isolated. I was interviewed by the YMCA to get a place in a hostel and upset them by saying I was a stranger in a strange land. They gave me a place on condition that I get help. I helped myself by leaving after a few weeks and got a bedsit which made me feel worse. Then I started to go to gay pubs and clubs. The places I went to were badly furnished, the drink was expensive and they were mainly picking-up places for one-night stands which I didn't want and I found that I would start to panic after a few minutes. I didn't like being in crowds or being touched up by people who just wanted to use me sexually, so I stopped going to such places. I find, as I did then realize, a difference between love and affection and lust too much to cope with. I didn't at the time know any gay people who I could just socialize with so it was very difficult. I read a lot of gay books, both fiction and non-fiction. Television had its own warped view of very camp or promiscous gays so that didn't help and if Wolfenden helped it took some years to percolate through. In the meantime I decided that socialism was the only way to equality and I was very conscious of rejecting the label 'homosexual' as I felt that there was, and is, more to people than generalized labels, and I couldn't think what a homosexual or a queer or a fairy was.

COLIN

All I can recall about my early sexual exploits is that they were done in secret. From early childhood, playing around with other boys seemed right. My first experiences were with an older boy who showed me his penis and asked me to play with it. I did, and I enjoyed it. He would then reciprocate. Not all the boys joined in with our group who liked to play sexual games. It seemed OK because the older boys did it. So we were safe and no one would say anything. I recall an occasion when this one young boy and me were alone together and I took all his clothes off. I tried to have sex with him, but he didn't want to. I guess, looking back, you could say I had raped him.

As I grew older and became aware that homosexuality wasn't something people openly showed and understood, I had to hide many of my feelings and emotions. Thankfully I had one friend at school who was gay like myself. We were able to talk and share with each other. He became my only sexual partner also. However, my attitude began to change and I began to get depressed about my homosexuality. I was annoyed that I had to keep my emotions and feelings suppressed because of other people's lack of understanding. I wasn't enjoying sex and my partner knew this. So he went elsewhere.

For the next five or six years I hid in a closet fighting the fears within, turning to masturbation and dreams. I started work at seventeen and began mixing with new people. I got involved in a youth group and started to have an active social life with 'straight' people. Yet I was never physically attracted to females, except maybe one in a million. It was at these youth meetings that I met my next lover. I was attracted both physically and sexually. He was tall, dark and well-built. From then on I was able to accept my homosexuality and express it as openly as I could without offending those around me.

DON

It's funny, but I think my first feelings about homosexuality and sexual arousal was a strong urge to keep it secret forever. I definitely knew the name for it. I was twelve. My parents tuned into a wonderful radio show called *Round the Horne* every week. I adored Kenneth Williams as Sandy with his 'friend' Julian, obviously a gay couple. I loved the camp sense of humour, it sort of felt part of me. Otherwise the images of homosexuality were negative: the *Daily Express* which my parents took, anti-gay banter by my schoolmates who somehow sensed I was gay without telling them. One incident: in the changing-room two older boys, sixth formers, came into the showers. I was amazed by the size of their penises and their gloriously profuse pubic hair. I was simply overwhelmed with amazement and rushed out into the changing room and called to my friends to come and look. They must have thought I was mad. Forever after they taunted me. If I was walking past the changing-room they would pull down their pants and make obscene thrusts with their hips. I was a laughing stock. This was my first lesson in the art of concealment.

There were a few inspiring moments, like seeing Little Richard circa 1970 on *The Old Grey Whistle Test* demonstrating how he put on his lipstick; a documentary about Christopher Isherwood who had an unbelievably high-pitched camp voice; seeing David Bowie for the first time on *Top of the Pops*, amazingly androgynous and camp. And wicked. On the other hand the hateful and despicable Danny La Rue represented the other side of the coin. He seemed to be on television all the time.

Within myself I treasured my secret. From the age of twelve onwards I masturbated every day and had wonderful fantasies about sex with other men. My own wonderful orgasms made me feel homosexuality was OK, nothing outside did.

The first homosexuals I ever met were in the sixth form at school. Jeannie and Beth were lesbians. Everyone knew this. It was unspokenly tolerated. Because of my secret I thought they were wonderful! A small circle of us formed around them, and we went to their bedsit every night when we left school in 1974, five or six of us. We drank cider or Martini because it was cheap, listened to Led Zeppelin, smoked dope, grew our hair long and popped all the pills we could lay our hands on. Terry, a fat and unhappy closet queen, kept us supplied. He had a fairly serious drugs problem – slimming pills, downers, codeine and so on. My next-door neighbour, also eighteen, was a close companion. I didn't find out he was gay until five years later (and I didn't tell him until ten years after that) when he met me off the train from university and told me he was living with a man.

All the time I was at university I kept my homosexuality a secret, but had some gay friends. Quite a few people thought I was gay. All my windows were smashed by my fellow students but I kept my 'secret'. I dropped out of university – partly too much dope, devoting too much time to the student newspaper, depression, just my isolation as a homosexual. Straight friends supported me through my crisis. We got drunk and stoned together. I lost my virginity to a woman in the collective next door. While in bed with her I told her I wanted to make love to her boyfriend. She persuaded him to join us in bed and the three of us made love together. I noticed he wasn't particularly good at homosexual sex! I felt love for him but couldn't talk to him about it. I slept with him once more a year later, again on his girlfriend's orders. It was a sympathy fuck and not that wonderful. He failed to excite me to orgasm. I fell in love with another straight man. He slept with me once, swearing me to secrecy. We could never talk about it. I suppose this situation lasted for five or six years. I saw him every day. He was my drug-dealer as well as my best friend. In the end I couldn't stand it any more and moved to London. It was all very unhappy, largely due to the fact that I wouldn't come out as homosexual. Deep within me I treasured my secret, but most of me was unhappy. I feel rejected by the homosexual community. Men, I feel, do not find me attractive. I long for a relationship with a man, but find myself unable to achieve this. I'm now thirty-three. It is hell being single all these years.

PHILIP

My awareness of my sexuality occurred over such a long period and so slowly that it can't be pinpointed. Say between nine and nineteen. There was never any period of angst. I just accepted slowly that I liked men and didn't like women. This was academic until after a short period in the army during the war, at eighteen and-a-half, I became friendly with a homosexual man in the same camp. He did a lot of explaining of what homosexuality was and that that was what I was. He was about twenty-two years old, very intense, artistic and a beautiful pianist. He had had some experience himself. But until I was sent overseas to India at nineteen, I still had not had an adult experience.

I quickly fell in love with India, learning the language and consorting far more with the natives, civilian and military, than with my own. One day, walking in the country with two Indian friends I had met earlier on, we walked hand in hand which was a common custom and didn't necessarily mean anything sexual. Anyway the excitement of so doing gave me an erection and I pertly pointed this out to them. Result: we found a copse of trees. Dropping my pants I was taken by them in turn. I didn't see their genitals and felt no discomfort. However, the discovery of the ease with which it was possible to find sex of however brief a nature was illuminating, and I pursued my way, still in the Far East, for the next three years with exuberance. My companions were always Indians and of my choosing rather than theirs. Usually these were brief episodes in the woods or country lanes, but just occasionally a whole night in my partner's house. I was always the passive partner; probably this was the only way in which they would be interested. They were mostly what we would call ambisexual, and being Muslims (or Sikhs, a special case) with no access to females, took their sex where it chanced. Only on a very few occasions was I certain that my partner preferred the male.

My sexual role didn't change until my return to England at about twenty-three years old, and my first experience of sex with an Englishman. I found I much preferred the active role but all my life I have been quite flexible and respond to my partner according to *his* needs.

So my sexual awakening was very slow and it was many years before the concept of love began to dawn. I was well into my thirties before I had a liaison of any length of time with a man, and into my late fifties before I met two men with whom I am just about bigamous, one of whom I love.

DENNIS

My father died when I was ten years old, but owing to the war and his being in the army I hardly knew him anyway. Although he had fathered six children he had a real dislike of them and boys in particular so my world had always been dominated by my mother and sisters, as my older brothers were also away in the forces.

When I was eleven I met a man much older than me, probably in his fifties. Some would accuse him of seducing me, but I clearly remember willing him to show interest in me. I met him several times over the next seven years. From then on I was determined to meet more older men as I enjoyed meeting and being with them and that set a pattern for the rest of my life.

When I was seventeen I was arrested by the police when having sex in a cottage with another man and this completely changed my life, more than merely being gay could ever have. I was immediately expelled from school by my very religious headmaster. I was put through a County Court trial and placed on probation for two years. My mother, initially, found it difficult to adjust to the homosexual nature of my offence – 'Why couldn't you have got a girl into trouble?' – but did her best to support me. She arranged for me to attend a psychiatrist for treatment – this was part of the probation order – where, even at that fairly innocent age and in the anxious mood I was in, I could not help but be amused by the treatment. As my mother was not very well off I was pronounced 'cured' after two visits. I got the distinct impression that had we been better off the treatment would still be going on thirty-five years later. I did come out of this with a very negative view, imposed by others, of homosexuality.

My entire life seemed to have been ruined. I had always hoped to be an architect and had shown considerable promise, but expulsion from school meant that further study was impossible. So I went to work as an insurance broker, then as an architectural assistant and then as a travel clerk.

By this time the stress of my arrest and all her other worries resulted in my mother suffering an incapacitating stroke and I had to embark on a life on my own. I was eighteen by this time and my earnings were only enough to pay the rent on a small basement bedsitter, but not enough for food. Luckily for me a colleague, who appeared very glamorous to me, though not attractive sexually, suggested that I might join him at night working in a coffee bar. This solved the food problem and introduced me to the gay bedsit life of London W2 in the late 1950s. I realized there were others like me and that I could make friends and feel at ease with others like me without any sex. I always wanted closeness with older men, not with people of my own age. In later life I have had two long-term relationships, both with men thirty years my senior. The first lasted until his death after sixteen years of being together, and the present one still holds after twelve years.

I had to take early retirement as I was informed by a sympathetic superior that I had no chance of promotion and would always be pushed back because I was gay. This was in the cabin crew of a major airline where there are numerous gays in the operational ranks, but none should aspire to managerial status as I had. Even now I am still paying for my 'misdemeanour' at seventeen. I have now applied for several part-time jobs and been turned down because there was a possibility that I might have contact with and therefore be a danger to young people. Presumably my record was revealed during checks with the police which are permissible in such circumstances despite the Rehabilitation of

Offenders Act. I had asked for positions as a French language tutor, as an ambulance driver for disabled people and I currently expect to be turned down for a position as a mobile librarian for the same reason. The hetero-world is bent on lifelong revenge!

FRANK

Both in my later years at primary school and from the start of secondary school I engaged in genital play with some of the other boys. I can remember talk about local woods and commons where it was unsafe to go alone because of 'dirty old men', but I do not remember connecting their activities with our own. In the secondary school the gym master gave sex education to the fourth formers. He mentioned homosexual affections and activities as features of a passing phase through which some boys went; he was non-judgemental if I remember accurately.

About the time I was fourteen some boys older than I were expelled for sex in the underground bike-sheds. In reporting the expulsions at assembly the head was severely denunciatory, but imprecise. In the fifth form some friends and I discovered the writings of Oscar Wilde. I think this was through an interest in Bernard Shaw and his writings on socialism causing us to read Wilde's *Soul of Man Under Socialism*. We then read such books as there were about Wilde in my home town's rather good public library. Alec Waugh's *Loom of Youth* was reissued as a Penguin in 1941 and (perhaps rather absurdly when one considers the differences between our experience in our local day school in World War II with his experience in a boarding-school in World War I) it somehow helped some of us in our understanding of our attitudes towards and our relations and acts with each other; so did Compton Mackenzie's *Sinister Street* about a boy at a day school. Apart from the headmaster's speech about the expulsions I do not remember any denunciations of homosexual activity; on the other hand, we kept ourselves to ourselves, so to speak, and were well aware of the risks we ran. I do not recall any discussion of sex with my parents.

At eighteen-and-a-half I became a student. My eyesight was too poor for me to be called up. Chiefly through shyness in a very different environment but partly because of the very disrupted social life in my university at the end of the war and start of peace, I did not enter into whatever gay life there was there.

But I read voraciously in English and French and what I read confirmed the positive view of my own condition which I had already formed.

Soon, however, press reports began to make it clear how hostile the law and the courts were. This was particularly true in my first years in my first job in the early 1950s. Yet the society in which I chiefly mixed as a teacher in a civic university was remarkably tolerant and, although the expression was not used or, at any rate, was not known to me, I came out to straight friends and immediate colleagues in the spring of 1954 when there were parliamentary debates which led to the appointment of the Wolfenden Committee.

NICK

Although I started masturbating regularly when I was eleven or twelve I had in fact tried it when I was five or six or maybe slightly younger, and the impulse behind these attempts was definitely homoerotic. I think that I must have been disturbed by what I did because I told my mother and said it 'felt funny'. She gently told me not to do it and I followed her advice for about six years.

I suppose I was fourteen or fifteen when homosexuality was raised during a Religious Education lesson at school. All the details now escape me but I have a feeling that homosexuals were painted as pathetic (in the true meaning of the word) figures of fun. My reaction: No, surely not me. My history textbooks gave me an inkling that James I was homosexual but how it depressed me to read the adjective 'ridiculous' applied to his male favourites.

Our RE lessons dealt with general moral principles, not with particular cases. With the aid of these lessons I evolved what seemed to me to be a satisfactory moral code. I had been given homosexual feelings; these were morally neutral; as long as I remained chaste I would not be breaking the moral law. In retrospect, I think I might express this moral code differently. As long as I did not engage in any homosexual acts, and thereby offended neither the Church nor God, nobody would have any just cause for getting at me. I just hoped that nobody would discover that I masturbated. I was turning into a real closet case.

Our priest-teacher told us, in RE lessons, not to masturbate, otherwise it would become a habit. Were we to reach the stage of masturbating once a day the habit would become well-nigh unbreakable. Masturbation, we were told, was a serious sin, serious enough to bar us from heaven. To receive such instruction at the age of fifteen when I had been masturbating frequently for three or four years seemed to me to display gross negligence on the part of the school; they ought to have told me much earlier. With no intention of doing evil of any sort I was condemned to hell. How could this be? It could not be right. It was unbelievable. It was wrong, wrong, wrong.

On one occasion, when I was in the fifth form, a teacher publicly ridiculed two boys who had been discovered in a toilet cubicle together. This made me angry inside. There was another boy in my class who was reputedly gay. We were acquaintances, nothing more. Unfortunately he was the butt of many unkind remarks. I could never see why because I knew nothing out of the ordinary about him. When we got into the sixth form he was attacked by several boys in the sixth-form room. I came in at the tail-end of the incident so I only witnessed his escape. I became angrier and withdrew further into myself.

In class one day, a pupil asked another priest-teacher if homo-sexuality was wrong. Instead of giving us a proper and reasoned yes or no, the priest said, 'Most homosexuals commit suicide.' We had been taught that suicide was a mortal sin and the infer-ences were obvious. I was doubly furious. He had said, in effect, that homosexuality is wrong, but he had drawn no distinction betwen orientation and action, and he had used what I believed then and believe now to be a lie to condemn us. By the time I finished my formal schooling I do not think I had seen one instance where homosexuality was positively portrayed and I knew no other homosexuals *per se*. During my time at college (1966–9) the public debate preceding the 1967 Act must have, I suppose, provided some positive support for me. But within weeks of the Act a technical assistant had been sacked from the college for a homosexual act while celebrating his twenty-first birthday in his own flat.

I was so naive about homosexuality that it took me ages to realize that Julian and Sandy in *Beyond Our Ken* and *Round the Horne* were meant to be gay. When I found out I enjoyed them even more. After I left college I began to read things in the *Observer* which mentioned something called the Gay Liberation Front. My heart leapt for joy. We were fighting back at last.

And when I made my first visit to London and made my way to Kensington High Street and saw little GLF stickers on lamp-posts, I was over the moon. But I still did not get to meet anyone gay.

On my next visit I attended a GLF disco at a pub on the south side of the Thames by Putney Bridge. Oh, what a disappointing looking lot they were. The one chap I actually talked to was a real turn-off. I was too scared to dance. I was shy, of course, but I was terrified of being drawn into 'forbidden' areas and of being discovered and punished by . . . by what? I fled after only a short time, but even before I reached the north bank of the Thames I was bitterly regretting my cowardice. To be gay meant to be brave.

From this point I entered a period of increasing despair. We had been made for love; everywhere around me, in books, television, church and music, love was proclaimed; yet here I was, unloved, forbidden to love and *unable* to love. Why did I think unable? Because I had read a book called *The Erotic Minorities* in which it was stated that, alone of all these minorities, fetishists could not develop satisfactory relationships. I had discovered, too, that Tchaikovsky had been gay, but his death was possibly suicide. Was my priest-teacher right? Was I going to kill myself? I think that I learned of the existence of the Campaign for Homosexual Equality (CHE) from small ads. I joined, and learned of the existence of Friend but, despite my increasing despair, did not make contact for some considerable time. In the meantime I battled on and shouted and screamed at the gates of heaven. And then, remembering the quite serious advice we received from a priest-teacher at school that God helps those that help themselves, I contacted Friend. Finally, in my mid-twenties, I met pleasant and interesting gay people and I found a lover. Joy. Relief. Disbelief. I had been taught in RE lessons that God does not answer in the affirmative any prayers which might not be to the good of the petitioner. My prayers for love had been answered in the affirmative. Joy. Internal conflict. Confusion.

From that day to this I have maintained that love between two people of the same sex is a good and beautiful thing. It is something I would like to enjoy again but my belief in the positive good of gay love is not at all strong. My belief has weakened at times, especially because of my job as a teacher. I have found that being fully, actively gay and being a teacher is incompatible and I have divorced myself from gay life. In the process I have occasionally discovered that I was internalizing modes of thought and accepting premises which were ultimately anti-gay. It was to counteract these vile influences that I maintained my membership of CHE, subscribed to *Gay News* and *Gay Times*, joined the Gay Bookclub and joined Quest. Recently Quest has had a local revival and it is already brightening my landscape so that I am, once again, becoming able to see my homosexuality in a positive light.

IAN

I think I was about fourteen or fifteen, masturbating regularly and fully aware of most aspects of sex from books and friends, although not from personal experience, before the school authorities told us anything about sex and that was pretty pathetic in divinity classes at school, about seeds and wombs. This was not in the 1950s but in the early 1970s at an all-boys minor public school. I learned nothing about sex from my parents either, though once my father handed me a little booklet actually entitled *The Birds and the Bees* (true!), very embarrassed, saying, 'Mum wanted me to give this to you.' It was well-meant but far too little – not a bit explicit – far too late. I think it didn't say anything about homosexuality.

No, I learned about homosexuality initially from a schoolfriend called David who sat next to me at school. He had rather liberal parents who had told him the facts of life which he passed on to me. Once I realized how innocent I was and how all this had been kept from me I read all I could about sex, though mostly rather tedious pieces in *Encyclopaedia Brittanica* and the like!

I had absolutely no sexual experience with anyone else until I was sixteen when I had sex with a teacher at school. There had been a few pseudo-sexual experiences at cub and scout camps, when I was between nine and eleven, which I had found exciting – strip-poker games with older scouts, the sound of a boy I had a crush on peeing outside the tent I lay in, the rumours that an older bully had stripped a cub and made him lick his boots in submission. Of course I had no idea what all this meant, but I knew by instinct or early training that it was something to keep quiet about.

I was intensely unhappy during my early teens for no obvious reason, and I often fantasized about suicide. I think this was connected with knowing, semi-consciously, that I was gay and that I would probably never fit in at school and feeling isolated from other children. I was bullied by my older brother who, by irony, has also turned out to be gay, and felt misunderstood and perhaps even unloved by my parents. There was no physical contact, no caressing or hugs and few kisses.

A strong element throughout all this period was the Catholic church. I went to confession regularly from the age of eight onwards. This was in the 1960s before the practice of going to confession became less popular or frequent. Between eight and twelve I went every two to three weeks. From about twelve onwards I think I always brought up sex in confession as I had to bring up masturbation – the indoctrination was effective – and often mentioned that I was, or feared I was, homosexual. I went to a number of different priests and received varying reactions. None was very encouraging. All regarded it at least as an aberration to be fought against with prayer and, in at least one case, sports and other distractions. I was not in the least sporty. One told me that he had known many homosexuals but none had been happy. I was told this when I was about fourteen and it haunted me for a long while. My views about priests remain rather negative as a result of this. By the time I was eighteen I felt much better about being gay and since then have not really had moral feelings about it. I know it isn't wrong whatever anyone else says so it doesn't bother me, except it sometimes makes me angry when people say it is incompatible with Christianity and so forth. I have not been to confession since I was twenty-one although I remain in other senses a practising Catholic.

A seminal experience (in several senses!) came when I was sixteen. I had confided my homosexuality to the teacher I had a crush on – perhaps 'was in love with' would be more accurate. He reacted in a neutral but not sympathetic way and shied away when he realized I was getting too attached to him. Without my permission he told two other members of the staff about me. One of these who was actually a minister of religion, though not Catholic, however, approached me and was quite sympathetic. We had little chats in a deserted classroom after school. During one of these he put his arms round me and we had sex by body-rubbing. I felt excited, but very confused and upset about it all.

I didn't really fancy him but welcomed any experience of physical affection. We had sex on a number of other occasions and he discreetly introduced me to other gay people. This snowballed and by the time I was eighteen I felt much better about being gay. I was reading the fairly new gay publications like *Gay News* and had access to more positive images of gay life. I am glad to be gay, well about 95 per cent of the time.

GRAHAM

At primary school I was unbelievably popular with the girls, often the only boy at their parties. My domesticity – being good in the kitchen and fond of knitting and of being practical with my younger brother and sister – was well known. By the time I was eleven I found some boys attractive physically. The images I had picked up by then were mixed. I was teased, but in a gentle, mostly affirming way, about my 'cissyness'. We are not a very macho family, my father being older than most and having been treated badly as a POW, was very gentle with us. Being middle class and fairly intellectual neither of my parents were very doctrinaire with us about anything.

At an all-boys grammar school, homosexuality was nothing one could own up to. The RE master was the butt of all scorn on this score. Another master behaved towards me in what I thought at the time was a peculiarly open way. I could get away with anything during his classes, but the hatches were well and truly battened down on my sexuality by then. I fancied boys in my class and had fantasies about them; likewise in my scout troop. How I longed for girls to share with! Only by the sixth form did I discover that some other boys were bisexual, if not gay. But by then I was so scared of my own tendencies that I did not share anything with them. I had fallen into the general gay-knocking mentality of the school which I trusted more than my feelings and attractions. This was also reinforced by my perception as a Christian that homosexuality, probably as orientation and certainly in practice, was sinful. Having said this, my father encouraged us in Anglo-Catholicism where there was far more drama and mysticism than dry moral teaching. One priest in my adolescence was friendly and we were fond of each other. In retrospect I suppose he could well have been gay.

After a stressful time as a member of a congregation where

there was a gay clique with which I was friendly but disapproving it took me until I was at theological college to accept my homosexuality. The signals there were fairly mixed but I was helped by some of the priests on the staff and one or two fellow students, including the one I fell for. There was a lot of camp behaviour there, and it was acceptable, if not desirable, to be gay. Basically undergirdled by care, here was somewhere secure I could slowly examine my feelings and tendencies. Only there did people give me a lot of time and help to talk about my very real feelings.

WILLIAM

As a child I never really enjoyed the things that boys are supposed to enjoy. I preferred Sindy to Action Man. I didn't play with those Airfix sets of plastic soldiers in the garden and I hated playing cricket or football. I was often the only boy invited to girls' parties when they were shunned by my contemporaries as being cissy. In the playground I sometimes played skipping or elastics with the girls, comforted by the fact that footballers skipped as part of their training. I was not aware of any animosity towards me from others in my class.

A couple of us once went round the playground asking various other children if they were 'a homo'. If they replied 'No', we sneered and said, 'But aren't you homo sapiens?' and if they answered, 'Yes', we sneered and said, 'Ugh, you're a homosexual!' Children can be so cruel. In first-year juniors one of my friends had one of those novelties which is a tube with pictures of naked women inside, and when you looked down it you got a ring of black ink around your eye. Although I never got to look down it I remember stating quite forcibly that I preferred pictures of naked men. However, at that tender age I didn't put two and two together and I don't think any of my friends did either.

Although I have had homosexual feelings since my early teens I have only recently, at eighteen, fully accepted and come to terms with my homosexuality. Previously I had thought that some day I would get married and have children. I used to go through phases of liking a particular name such as Ryan or Sindy or Greg or Nigel and deciding that one of my offspring would be called that. Nowadays when I say that I will never marry and have children I find that I can't give the reason why. I haven't told anyone about my homosexuality yet as there never seems to be a right time. Recently, when I told my mother that there were some things I didn't feel I could tell her, I felt I might not ever be able to tell her. The turning-point in regard to my feelings about my gayness was when I bought the August 1985 copy of *Gay Times*. I read it from cover to cover and afterwards I felt an upsurge of feeling. I was actually glad to be gay. However, although inside me I wanted to shout it out from the rooftops, I knew I couldn't and wouldn't be able to. Secrecy, I think, is one of the worst aspects of being gay.

ALAN

I was eight years old when a male school friend showed me his bare bottom in the boys' toilets. I was fascinated, because it was rude and I enjoyed it. I remember it vividly. A couple of years later I visited my classmate's home and his fifteen-year-old brother joined us. Their parents were out and we played 'Strip Jack Naked'. When we were all naked the older brother insisted on forfeits. Each forfeit was to touch and stroke a part of another person's body. It began with head, legs, arms and chest. When it came to the genitals I was frightened by it. My fear was that it was rude. I had never seen my parents naked. I had been brought up to believe that genitals were very private and intimate parts. I told my mother. She reacted well and said I need not visit again if I didn't want to.

At the same time there was a playground game called 'cannon-ball' whereby you grabbed other boys between the legs, squeezing their genitals. I disliked the pain, but some boys were gentle and I enjoyed that immensely. At eleven I finally stripped with a local friend during the summer behind some disused garages and we rolled about together in the grass. I then knew that I liked the male sex and considered it to be natural.

At high school I began having heart-throbs. I was twelve and it was the year of my first orgasm. One day, at breaktime, a boy in my class ran up to me and, without venom or malice, said 'You're a queer.' I asked him to explain. He said, 'You like boys', and ran off. This was never uttered again but I began to think about being a homosexual. Shortly after that incident my mother gave me a small booklet written for the scouts. It said that interest in other boys was a phase and usually went away when you were fifteen. I was over the moon. After all, everyone I knew was heterosexual. Weren't they?

At fourteen I went on holiday with my parents and my cousin to Belfast. We visited friends one day just outside Dublin, on a farm. There were masses of children. We were sent out to play. We jumped on haystacks, the girls screamed, we rolled through the grass. Then suddenly one boy and I walked into grass so tall that only our heads peeped over the top. As we walked his brown whirlpool eyes and velvet accent made me feel very strange. He suddenly took hold of my hand. I believe that was the first time I have ever fallen in love. So much so that my recollections are of a dreamlike quality. It was one of the most beautiful experiences of my life.

I began to worry from then on about when I would start fancying girls. I was shy and clumsy with them, or so it seemed to others. In fact I treated them as sisters. At fifteen my family moved a good hundred miles away. I hated my new school. One day my mother showed me a newspaper article about a man who had interfered with young boys. For weeks I was in horror of turning out like him. I decided to give myself until my sixteenth birthday and, if I hadn't turned heterosexual, would commit suicide. I had thought of suicide on and off since the age of thirteen, but they were only half thoughts. This time it was for real.

Friends of my parents moved abroad. They had a son of my age who was left at public school in England and visited his parents only for the summer and Christmas holidays. All other holidays were spent with us. We shared a twin bedroom. He sneaked in copies of a girlie magazine. The naked women did nothing for me, in fact I found some of them rather sickening, but the stories describing the men were sensational. We would both read by torchlight. One night he invited me to his bed. That began a long series of sexual discoveries. We shared body rubbing, masturbation, oral sex both ways and eventually he attempted anal intercourse on me but it was too painful. I found the pleasure of our relationship to be wholesome, but a secret from the whole world. After all, it was taboo. He would never kiss me. He said, 'That's what girls do.'

Eventually he left to join his parents and my family moved to London. I studied hard for the first year at college, but the nagging questions about my homosexuality affected my later studies. I told a few college friends that I was gay and it was accepted, but I knew no one else who was gay. Relatives were continually pushing me towards obtaining a girlfriend. I had a few, but when they started making sexual advances towards me I ditched them. I became depressed and, for the first time, discovered that gays could be found in public lavatories. At first I thought the whole business horrendous, but I was totally intrigued. Eventually I got more daring and performed sex acts in public. It was quick satisfaction and anonymous. It was fun. As a horny seventeen-year-old I couldn't get enough. I was on the road to promiscuity.

That year, 1967, the Sexual Offences Bill was passed. I was still under age. I spread my wings and travelled from loo to loo searching. Of course what I wanted was someone to talk to. My college friends, family and other friends flaunted their heterosexuality. Sexual gratification wasn't enough. I went to my doctor and asked for a sex change. I was depressed, I wanted to commit suicide and I had homosexual tendencies. He advised a psychiatrist.

Between then and my first appointment a college friend spoke to her parents saying she was afraid I was going to kill myself. They in turn phoned my parents. My father visited me at college. I came out. It was such a relief to me, but a shock to them.

The first visit to the psychiatrist was my last. He said I was gay and I decided to save my parents the fees by talking things out with them. It took me a while to chip away at my parents' misconceptions. My mother feared I would be a child molester hanging around public lavatories, in and out of prison, dressed up as a woman, being attacked by queerbashers, never getting a decent job and being discriminated against for the rest of my life. It took them three or four years to come to terms with my sexuality.

It took the same length of time for me to join GLF and to understand to some degree the reasons for homophobia, the fear of their own homosexuality. My greatest learning came from older gays who had been through the hard years. I was on the wave of the permissive society. They helped me prise open the closet door.

GARETH

I remember, at the age of six or seven, watching with my father the professional boxing on television and becoming excited seeing the men's half-naked bodies. Another pleasurable sexual memory was when in the infants school an older boy put his T-shirt over my head in the playground lavatories one day. I felt the warmth of his chest against my face and this was very exciting. From my first year in secondary school, infatuations with other boys were a regular occurrence. Various boys in my class began to taunt me about being queer. I don't know whether they really had any evidence for this or just a feeling. I felt deeply unhappy and wanted to change schools.

When I was about fourteen I found somewhere an old copy of *Private Eye* with contact advertisements in the back. I began corresponding with a man from London. I telephoned him to arrange to go up one weekend. In the meantime my parents found the letters and summoned one of their friends, the deputy headmaster of the local reformatory school. He gave me a lecture, telephoned the man in London and threatened him with the police if he tried to contact me again.

The following year I changed schools at last and was much happier in a single-sex grammar. It was with great reluctance that my parents allowed me to join the National Youth Theatre youth group with whom I had won a place in London the following summer. To my surprise I was approached by various men in Trafalgar Square and went home with one of them. After that I ran away from home to London the following half-term and in the Christmas holidays. London seemed magical.

When I was in the sixth form I began to see a third former who happened to be head chorister in the local cathedral and had the lead in the school musical. One weekend when he had been invited down my mother found us in bed together. 'If his father finds out he'll kill you,' she said. There were many other incidents like this. I used to reply to ads in *Gay News* and men would sometimes visit, always conspicuous in our village. Relations with my parents hit an all-time low and there was violence between my father, my brother and me. Despite this, my homosexuality was never openly discussed. Instead I was blackmailed emotionally, given coded warnings to conform if I wanted to remain in the same house.

It will come as no surprise that many times I wished I was straight. There were times when I prayed to wake up next morning straight. How much more convenient! All in all I was presented with negative images of homosexuality during these years. No one encouraged me, quite the reverse. At the single-sex school everyone who later turned out to be gay pretended not to be. For example, my cousin, who in all his adult life has lived with various male partners, used to take out girlfriends and deny his homosexuality. There were many others. Those who remained in the area were derided when it became known they were gay.

Looking back, it's a miracle that Stonewall ever happened. Perhaps it could only have happened in the US, certainly not in Wales! Only American gays could have had the strength and courage to fight back against all that shit.*

VICTOR

My earliest awareness of homosexuality was probably when, at the age of eight or nine, my older brother came back from boarding-school with extraordinary tales of what happened there. He was quite derogatory about the people who had been caught having anal and oral sex, and I suppose I was shocked too because it did not seem physically possible to me.

Before, and during, my early years in boarding-school I decided to learn as much as I could about sex from magazines, porn novels and videos which my father kept in his shirts drawer. I was a mine of information on the workings of the sexual organs, both male and female, and a precocious authority on orgasms and dating. Looking back now I can see I was very camp and obvious but with absolutely no direction.

I was ten when I started at a more liberal boarding-school. I cried a lot and was generally considered a great wimp, so the threat of anyone finding out that I liked to play with other boys was just another piece of aggravation I could live without. There were one or two boys I played around with and that was getting to prove unsatisfactory because it was not a progression. All my friends were dating and having sex with girls and I felt I wanted

---

* Stonewall – the New York bar where, in 1969, the clientele, worn down by continual police harassment, fought back. The Stonewall riots are celebrated as the beginning of gay liberation internationally and are marked every year at the time of 'Pride'.

to do the same with a boy and, if not, with a girl. At this point I met a boy much older than me, sixteen plus to my thirteen, who had a reputation for being a persistent wet-dreamer. It was a great revelation because we did all those stupid things that heterosexuals take for granted. He carried my bag and books, bought me cokes and, once in a while, crossed the dining-room to sit with me. I have little idea now what we must have talked about, but I get the feeling of having been desired more than just physically. I was aware that I wanted him sexually but, because he was older, I left the decision to him. One night he insisted I walk with him to his dormitory. He was very quiet and he held my hand which was reassuring. He stopped in some dark corner and asked how much I liked him. I tried to laugh it off with some vague reply but he persisted. My ears burned and my heart tripped as I said, 'A lot'. Then he kissed me and we went on and had sex. I remember thinking, this is all I want from life. He was quite strong and forceful and I remember him hitting a few people who made snide remarks, so for a whole year I felt loved and protected in the best of ways. I was so happy I did not notice my grades slide and my parents began to get worried. I missed him during the holidays, even more so because when friends and family told their tales of straight relationships I felt like a pressurized container, full of guilty secrets. In my fourth year I met another guy I fell deeply in love with even though nothing essentially sexual happened between us. We were very similar in backgrounds and attitudes, and he was very affection-ate. This led to a few spats with my previous boyfriend who did not like the idea of me 'sleeping around' which I wasn't. I was flattered but found it hard to decide where we went from that point so, after a very public fight, we stopped all communication. At the end of the fourth year my parents made me change schools and I ended up going out with a girl for a year. It was everything I wanted in a relationship with the knowledge of its possibilities and boundaries.

I started my A-levels and began to work on my attitude. For the next two years I never denied being a homosexual, though I did not admit to it. It was the peak period for Culture Club in the early eighties and I took to dressing a tiny bit outrageously when I could. It was such a boost to see Boy George flaunting his sexuality so defiantly. I also got 'Tainted Love' by Soft Cell and it seemed to sum up all the feelings I had at the time. It seemed, for the first time, that being a homosexual might involve more than just sex.

My first positive act was to write to London Friend after seeing some information about them in a listings magazine. I explained how I felt, about wanting to fall in love with another man and share and enjoy life with him to the full. I have kept to this day the letter I received. The guy who wrote it was very sensitive and positive, reminding me that I had to value myself and others, and to hold my head up no matter what. He explained that I was no different from anyone else because we all want to love, be loved and needed. At about this time gossip reached me that I had not been made a house prefect because of doubts about my sexuality and my friendship with some of the younger students. It was a blow because I was popular, my grades were about the best in the house and it was very obvious that I had been passed over. I ended up meeting the letter writer from London Friend who turned out to be a tall, thin man with hair dyed purple to orange, in make-up, eye-liner and black painted fingernails. He walked confidently. For me, on day-release from boarding-school, he totally freaked me out. I could see everyone pointing at me, going 'You are one of them.' I tried to get over the embarrassment and went to meet the group. They all looked so normal, confident, even bold. I was very surprised and relieved. These weren't guys who would run off to girlfriends in the morning. And they were happy being homosexual, something I carried away with me.

In my first week at university I took the great step of marching up to the Gaysoc desk at the Societies Bazaar. It was the strangest of years because almost everyone else was bisexual. I decided to come out to my best friend from boarding-school. Even though he was teased and called a poof a lot it never occurred to me that he was. On the fateful weekend I was beating about the bush and flicking through the personal columns in *Time Out*. Eventually I spat it out, 'I am gay', and shocked even myself. He laughed and said he was too and we became even better friends. We looked through the gay listings and called Gay Switchboard who recommended the nightclub Heaven. It was strange seeing so many men dancing together, some without shirts, in leather chaps and thongs, ripped jeans, kissing, hugging, loitering in toilets, groping one another. I felt the police would rush in and cart everyone of us off to some cell somewhere. I learned to relax on subsequent visits and ended up getting picked up by a guy and that was the start of a year-long affair.

BRYAN

From the age of about six or seven other kids began to call me poof. Everyone knew what a poof was, it was a man who shagged other men, and to be called one was considered, as it still is, the grossest kind of insult. I was the skinny boy who didn't play football – two counts of weirdness already – but I was well-liked and I had many friends. However, being the target of this verbal abuse was made all the more painful by the fact that I already did feel different from my friends. I was probably not loud enough, rude enough or tough enough for a boy, but I do wonder if I drew those insults as the result of obvious visible signals or if others could detect a difference in me with a more primitive sense.

What I am absolutely certain about is the first time I fell in love. I was seven years old. One day we had been playing in the playground and were about to go back indoors. I must have looked up or turned round, and I saw someone I had never seen before. There was a sudden lurch in my stomach. I was looking at the most beautiful boy I had ever seen. He stayed at our school for only a short while and I never learned his name. I did learn that he had previously lived in Germany, so when I went home I looked up my father's German–English dictionary and worked out a no doubt clumsy translation of 'I love you'.

And then he was gone. I would not experience that same intense sensation on seeing someone for a long time, and meantime my sexuality seemed a rather shapeless thing, burgeoning but utterly private. I knew that the feelings I had looking at other boys' bodies – a beautiful face, the curve of thighs and calves, suntanned skin under an unbuttoned white shirt – these things were taboo, but I never felt it was bad or wrong. Just awkward. How did these things fit in?

When I was about eight or nine a friend and I would sometimes show each other our cocks and, on two or three occasions, when we had an empty house, we would undress in front of each other, but we never touched.

At thirteen I discovered masturbation. When I brought myself to orgasm my head was filled with images of other boys, the school athletes or my close friends. I shared a bedroom with my younger brother and a number of times I would get into bed beside him at night. We would touch each other and I would get a hard-on and suck his cock and wank onto him. This was something new and exciting and the feeling of coming was astonishing. This only happened a handful of times, probably because he was not old enough to experience equal gratification. Solitary masturbation became my sole expression of physical sexuality.

I never felt bad or guilty nor did I feel any need for advice or help. The feelings in my body and the thoughts in my head were so good that I knew they had to be special, to be treasured.

I left home to go to college. There, my closest friend was a woman who, after a couple of weeks, asked me one day in her usual direct manner if I was gay. I said, 'Yes.' We both laughed. No one had ever asked me this before and my answer validated my sexuality in the real world. I decided to come out to my friends, many of whom had moved to the same city. They accepted my news, but I felt that by asserting my gayness I had set myself apart from them, moved beyond the limits of their world and, indeed, within a year I had lost contact with all of them. I told my parents when I was twenty-one, and not in the best circumstances. I was having an argument with my father, a battle of wits which seemed to evolve to the point where I, in exasperation, had to declare, 'Well, I'm homosexual!' I don't think they were too pleased but they seem to accept it now and the fact that I've lived with another man for the last five years.

Before I left home I had never knowingly met other gay people. The woman I met at college was, of course, a lesbian and she was probably the best person I could have met at that time. She was a strong and charismatic character whose honesty and passionate egalitarianism fired my sense of political identity and self-awareness. I must say that I have yet to meet a man who possesses such qualities.

I had always known there must be other gay people, other gay men, somewhere, but the only images I had come across were the same tired stereotypes on television. In books – encyclopaedias and family health dictionaries and so on – I must have looked up dozens of references to homosexuality, and I don't remember any positive descriptions. My sexuality was a disorder, a disfunction, an aberration, mental disturbance, perversion. Even the occasional call for 'tolerance' seemed to be an insincere attempt by the writer to seem 'modern'. I was both depressed and angered by these descriptions, so repetitive, so full of hate and revulsion really, and very similar in language and tone to, say, Nazi racist propaganda. What is important here is that I knew that these images – the 'poofters' on television, the sad and understandably lonely men in reference books – were not me, and, therefore, were not the others like me? It did not take me long to become aware that my sexuality made me part of a group which social consensus had decreed necessary to contain, control and, if and when possible, to eliminate.

2

Law

CHRISTOPHER

I have had contact with the police all my life as my father was in the force till he retired recently. This shaped my attitude in many ways; he tended to be rather right-wing in his views towards such things as race, the royal family, unions and so on, which drove me in the opposite direction so that I developed rather radical views, though I wouldn't describe myself as a social-ist. We disagreed about a lot of things without falling out. One thing which he turned me against was the elitist attitudes in the police force, the idea that they were above criticism and that anyone who did criticize them was a left-wing anarchist out to subvert the state. Even when quite young I had started to see the police as not quite the paragons of virtue they were made out to be, and his tirades confirmed this; if he could have these attitudes then others might as well.

My first sexual experience was in a cottage near where I worked. I was twenty at the time. I had gone into a cubicle to relieve myself when a foot appeared beneath the wall. I was both thrilled and shocked at the same time. Though not having heard of cottaging before, I instinctively knew what was happening. I didn't know how to cope with it at the time so I left quickly, but came back the next day to see if it happened again. Needless to say, it did and this time I was prepared to make contact. I didn't know what to do, but just imitated what the other person did. When a foot appeared I put mine near it, when it moved closer I did as well, and so on. When our feet touched a hand appeared and, although I wasn't quite sure what it was going to do I got down and let it hold my privates. This was my first sexual experience, a disembodied hand wanking me. It might sound a cliché but I had never experienced anything as pleasurable as that first orgasm, and I went back for more.

For about two years after that I was heavily, and more or less exclusively, into the cottage scene. I was still living with my parents who had no idea I was gay and I had no opportunity to make other homosexual contacts. Also I had no idea where to go and what to do if I made such contacts. I enjoyed the sex in the cottages most of the time, though when I got desperate for it I was rather indiscriminate. It was all fairly anonymous and I made no friends. Looking back I wish there had been someone who could have told me about the pubs and the clubs and the various gay social groups because the cottage scene was power-fully addictive, a source of excitement in an otherwise quiet life. Even today it remains attractive, despite the fact that my social life has widened considerably. I can't despise it without being a hypocrite but I wish it hadn't been the only gay scene in my earlier years.

On one occasion when I was cottaging in Baker Street under-ground station, I approached a guy at one of the stalls who showed interest and whom I followed out. When outside he put on an official voice, asking me if I was queer (his term). I was stunned and said I didn't know what he meant. He asked me was I a homosexual to which I said, 'Yes.' It turned out he was London Transport Police, and I was taken to their office and questioned. All I can remember from this was that he asked me if I had done it before. I lied and said, 'No.' He said that if he caught me again I would be arrested. Apparently, as he was the only officer present, he couldn't arrest me, only warn me. I was terrified out of my life and didn't go back for some time, though eventually I did as it was such a good cottage. On reflection what I did was stupid; he had uniform trousers and a civilian jacket on but I hadn't noticed this. I had got cocky.

The second time I encountered the police was again when cottaging, this time in Marylebone Station. I wasn't actually doing anything, but was just approaching someone when, out of the cupboard, came four or five uniformed men. At first I thought they were attendants coming out of an office, until one or two other uniformed men came down the stairs, saying we were under arrest. It was then obvious that the ones in the cupboard had been watching until something was going on and had signalled the others to come down. I was terrified, and sidled round the big central set of stalls and ran up the stairs for all I was worth. All the time I was expecting to feel a hand on my shoulder, but I didn't. I later realized that they probably hadn't seen me doing anything, so they let me go; either that or they had enough for their arrest quota and couldn't be bothered.

I was beginning to feel frustrated, wanting to do more on the gay scene but not knowing where to go. I read in the book *Alternative London* about various gay counselling groups, and having obtained Gay Switchboard's number I rang them up and described the kind of group I was after. They put me on to a befriending group which was run by gay guys experienced on the scene who helped to introduce newcomers like myself to other newcomers and to the pubs and clubs. This was one of the best things which could have happened to me as I now started to mix with a wide variety of gay people in non-threatening situations, and got to see a large number of the pubs and clubs for the first time. I was gradually coming out of my shell.

This went on for some time fairly prettily when the blow fell. I was arrested for cottaging. This was very traumatic for me. I was in the cottage of the Army and Navy store in Victoria. One minute I was having a quiet grope with some guy in the next cubicle and the next there was a banging on the door and a head appeared over the wall and a rough voice ordered me to come out; it was the security guard. I was handled rather roughly, particularly when I foolishly tried to make a run for it. I was told in no uncertain terms that if I tried again I would go head first down the stairs. In an office the other man and I were questioned. I said nothing but the other man kept attempting to leave which only increased the tension. I felt literally numb, my mind wouldn't function. From the store we were taken by a police van to the local station. I knew all the things I should and shouldn't do, and started by giving my name and address and nothing else. The officer went through the details of what I was supposed to have done and kept trying to get me to sign a statement. At no time were they unpleasant, just persistent. I asked for the one phone call I knew I was allowed, intending to ring Gay Switchboard in order to get a solicitor. However, I was told that I couldn't do this until I was charged, and they couldn't do that until I made a statement. I held out, realizing what they were trying to do, but they added that no solicitor would be available until after the New Year, this was New Year's Eve, and this really panicked me. I was terrified my parents would find out. If I confessed now, I thought, I would be out quickly and could concoct some reason for being late, but if I stayed in jail over the holiday. . . . It was also during this time that I was kept on my own in a cell. I could hear nothing and my watch had been taken away so I had no sense of time. This and the inherent tension of the situation softened me up and I agreed to make a statement, even though I knew in my heart of hearts that I shouldn't. I admitted what I had done, made a written statement and was fingerprinted and photographed. I, of course, asked them not to tell my parents or my employer; I am a civil servant. They agreed to this. However, when I gave my address, rather than check it on the electoral register as I had been told they would, they rang my parents and said I had been arrested, but not what for. When I came out they were there to meet me and I just burst into tears. I had not only the task of explaining that I was gay, but what I had been doing. This upset them a great deal, as you can imagine, and was the worst possible way I could come out to them. My father took it reasonably well even though he was in the police, but my mother was very shocked. I wanted the whole thing to be over as quickly as possible, so when I was arraigned before the magistrate and given the opportunity of being tried by a jury I declined as it would have prolonged my parents' and my anxiety and pain. I was fined £25.

However, that was not the end of it as a month or so later I was contacted by the Department's security section and given a telling-off, not only for what I had originally done, but also for not telling them about my conviction. So now I have two black marks on my record. I obviously didn't tell them, so I can only think the police did, despite their assurances that they wouldn't.

From that time on I have had no contact with the police at all, apart from occasionally seeing a gay police friend! I am rather ambivalent towards them I must admit. One, of course, hears many stories of police *agents provocateurs*, indifference to reports of crimes on gays and various kinds of harassment. Even allowing for exaggeration some of it must be true. I have also seen what they do on picket-lines, and even if half of that is true then it is obvious they are not to be trusted. Intellectually I tell myself that they can't all be thugs or anti-gay, but also I have a gut reaction which is rather different which says that people are often attracted to the job because they like wielding power, and that, even if they are reasonable sorts on joining, the previous ethos of 'the job right or wrong', of being there to maintain standards rather than the law, some of which I saw in my father, can warp minds and attitudes. Some, at least, of them seem to have forgotten that they are servants of the public, all the public, rather than a caste of guardians of public morality set apart from the rest of us; this is something they must relearn. I would have to think very hard before co-operating with them, weighing up the circumstances. If it was in a non-gay situation I probably would, as criminals have to be caught, but if it was in any major gay-related crime I would only do it after consulting one of the advisory bodies.

KEVIN

One of the things that most infuriates me is when older gays, as they were always doing in the 1970s, would hark back to the 'wonderful days before the law'. Everything changed for the better for all gay men in England over twenty-one when the law was changed in 1967. Those who had relished those days of fear of blackmail, of imminent arrest, of having one's life ruined and instant alienation from one's family had to have warped minds indeed.

As 1967 approached there was an increasing sense of freedom in the air. Contact ads began to appear in mainstream magazines. *Films and Filming* was a notable example and carried hundreds of gay personal ads every month in the early 1960s. There was a men's boutique in the Carnaby Street area called Carnaby Male. They brought out a line of men's underwear, briefs in various colours. Today they are everywhere, but until then men had worn bulky and unattractive underwear, forever white or off-white. The boutique manager knew his market, gays flocked to buy them, so much so that a leaflet was inserted in the packaging inviting the purchaser to join the Carnaby Male Club. For a small subscription one would receive a newsletter with contact ads. I don't quite remember how it was initially organized but I offered to illustrate each copy of the newsletter with a slightly erotic drawing. The organizer would send me a set of stencils and I would draw on them with a stylus and send them back to be typed up for mailing. Eventually Carnaby Male decided it wanted to distance itself from the organization – perhaps there had been complaints from straight men into fancy underwear – and from then on it was known as CMC. The only newsletter I still have includes a drawing I did poking fun at someone who had suggested CMC badges 'for instant recognition'. My drawing was of a cheeky sailor with his back to us, naked from the waist down. CMC is tattooed across his bum. The caption read 'How about CMC tattoos for instant recognition?'

I was a teacher in my first year, newly down in London from the north. Here I was in the theatre capital of the world and earning only £17 per week, and that included London weighting! There was no way I could afford to live and get to see the number of plays I yearned for. So, I advertised in the newsletter saying I would do individually commissioned drawings at a pound a time. It seemed a good idea. It was something I could do. It made contacts for me with other gay men. There was an erotic fulfilment in them. And I could finance trips to the theatre. I was never, at any stage, asked to do anything which could be considered hardcore. What people wanted was pictures of men together, naked and free, maybe with a semi-erection. Today when Tom of Finland's most graphic illustrations and Robert Mapplethorpe's explicit photographs are for sale in hardback in non-specialist shops, my drawings would appear quite innocuous.

I never did discover the chain of events which led to the arrival of the police at my digs. This was the spring of 1967; the law was not enacted until the July of that year. The police were still being vigilant in bringing to book men who had sex together. It was well known that if police went to someone's home to arrest him and his partner for having sex then the place would be searched. Address books would be taken and the individual's network investigated. It was on one such occasion that my drawings were discovered. I was charged with sending pornographic material through the mails, tried at a magistrates court and fined £160 plus £140 costs, not much theatre-going for me for a considerable time after that. The policemen who visited me were quite courteous and ignored the collection of pornographic magazines which I had. They told me it could have been much more serious had they charged me with using the Royal mails for conspiratorial purposes, then it could have been an Old Bailey case, and I could have suffered from the publicity. But there are always hack reporters in magistrates courts and there are slack days for the Sunday newspapers and I was fair game. 'Naturally' I resigned my teaching job.

I come from a police family. My brother is a policeman. I have a cousin long in the CID, an uncle who was a chief constable and another who was a special. As I was exceptionally tall as a child virtually every day someone would say, 'Is he going to be a policeman when he grows up?' If only for that reason I could never have joined up! It has always sickened me the way the police victimize gay men. Many of the things we can be 'done' for are victimless crimes between consenting adults. When their time could be better spent tracking down rapists and those guilty of other violent crimes against the person, policemen are hiding in public lavatories waiting to pounce should two men happen to come in and look at each other's penises. Promotion depends on the number of arrests made and young constables can easily bump up their promotional chances this way. A few years ago there appeared briefly in the Earl's Court area of London, the phenomenon of so-called pretty policemen. These were young constables, considered to be the kind attractive to gay men, who would go into the gay bars and cruising areas dressed in the right kind of gear, deliberately to entrap. It seems that under the law if you chat someone up and he then moves on and you chat someone else up then you can be arrested for 'persistently importuning for an immoral purpose'. The pretty police would work in pairs. One would chat someone up and move on; the other one would then move in, chat up and go off with the victim. An arrest would then be made away from the area. What kind of a police force actually creates a crime in order to harass a section of the society they are supposed to serve?

My only other run in with the law came in 1969. There used to be a cottage near Charing Cross station, and nearby what I seem to remember as an underground car park. If you met someone you fancied in the cottage, which was always very crowded at any time of day or night, it was easy to walk to the car park which, most of the time, was deserted. One day I met a really nice lad. He was nineteen, I was twenty-four. No great age difference for a heterosexual, but for a homosexual under the law all the difference in the world. He was waiting for a train and didn't have time to come back with me to my flat so I suggested the car park. We had a beautiful time together. There are those who think that such encounters can only be sordid. Not at all.

He was gentle and sensitive and caring and we were both the
richer for the encounter. When we emerged from the car park it
was all over, we were met by two policemen who said they had
seen us going into the car park and had waited for us to come
out. They separated us and questioned us as to what we had been
doing. I lied that I had been feeling sick and we had gone in
there so I could throw up. I don't know how it happened, perhaps
my voice carried, but the lad came up with the same story.
Anyway, eventually they brought us back together again and
gave us a warning not to have sex in public places, which we
both vigorously denied. Then, poetic justice! I was churned up
with terror at the thought of having to go through another outing
in the Sunday papers, plus a trial and a possible jail sentence for
having sex with an under-age partner. My stomach responded
and I actually threw up, some of the bile spilling over one of the
policeman's boots. Thus we proved our story, I was vindicated
and we went on our way. We parted very shortly afterwards
never to see each other again, but what hilarity accompanied our
farewells!

HARRY

Prior to the age of eighteen I believed that my sexual expression
was perfectly normal. It was at this time that I found myself
before the courts for the first time. I had been enjoying sexual
behaviour with other boys.

My first experience had been at thirteen years of age with a
boy of the same age. This was the first time I learned anything
about sex. He was my best friend. He had learned about masturbation at school and was passing the knowledge on. I recall this
as a very happy experience. Quite a few of my friends indulged
in homosexual behaviour. I was happy to share with them. I
don't know if any others turned out to be gay in adult life. My
mother guessed, so she says, when I was fourteen. She has never
accepted it and is still determined to get me 'cured'. My father
has had no dealings with me; he doesn't want to know. I sought
help from doctors, priests and the like and because of that it took
over twenty years for me to come to terms with being gay. They
all, without exception, told me, 'You don't have to be the way
you are. You can be cured.' I believed them, followed their advice
and treatment and ended up very unhappy indeed.

I feel that many people, especially parents, put pressure on the young gay person to change. Even today this kind of approach is common. Sadly, it is sometimes in the form of, 'Gay? Oh no you're not. If you're going to do that sort of thing then you are not living here. You get out.'

I believe that the age of consent should be sixteen. From my own life I know that I was set in my ways by then and from my observation of others it has been the same. Those who are only dabbling in it grow out of it anyway. Even highly sexually active young boys if they are not gay by nature grow out of this activity and turn to heterosexuality as they mature. Their experience has done them no harm. Indeed, some have actually benefited from the experience. Some parents of young lads have actually said to me, 'If my boy is going to do that sort of thing then I would rather know who he is with than not know. If he is with you we know he will not be harmed or abused. He is safe to grow up as he wishes and to grow out of it in due time if he is going to.' What a sensible, refreshing attitude. The law does not allow for such attitudes of course. As far as the law is concerned such lads are in need of care and protection and promptly puts them into 'care'. Fools – it does not stop sexual feelings and behaviour, it only increases those in danger of being harmed. You cannot legislate for emotions. What are MPs doing? Trying to hide *their* guilt behind a cloak of respectability? Of course they *never* did such things when they were younger! And certainly *none* of them would dream of doing it now. At least, no member of the Conservative Party! Ha! Ha! If only we knew! The only protection needed is for children of immature development, those below the age of puberty, also the mentally and physically handicapped. Boys and girls of normal growth and mental ability should be free to choose for themselves.

JAMES

I take the view that in any large and complex organization you are bound to get the occasional good apple. However, wherever they are in the barrel, good apples don't turn rotten ones back into good ones. The rot in our police force has well and truly set in and until someone finally succeeds in making the police accountable to the public, then not just gays but blacks, women, the homeless, the mentally ill, football supporters, anyone who isn't white, middle class and posh sounding is going to get a raw deal at the hands of an increasingly militarized, macho and moronic force.

I know of only two incidents worth mentioning about gays and the law. One concerns a close friend of mine trapped by a pretty policeman in a cottage. He went to the station and was politely treated. When questioned he gave his name and address only. He refused to give his fingerprints – the police had no right to take them – and to be photographed, but he was with a Polaroid camera. He managed, in spite of his fear, to do all this very politely. He was not charged with an offence but allowed to go home after being told he would get a summons in due course. He came straight to my house from the police station. We immediately wrote down every detail he could remember of what had happened. A mutual solicitor friend who specializes in cottaging cases agreed to represent him if necessary. My friend has a highly responsible job which he would certainly have lost if the case had gone against him. For six weeks he was inconsolably depressed. I've never known him so distressed and worried. Finally a communication arrived to say that the case was not to be pursued. I think he was lucky to be able to give the impression of being a relaxed, articulate and determined person. The police probably realized that there was no hope of getting a prosecution. If he had been taken to the magistrates court, he was prepared to have the case heard in a county court where he would certainly have won.

The other case comes from my work. A young student I had been counselling for homesickness, culture shock and a difficulty in personal relationships was assaulted one night in a certain park, well known as a cruising ground for gays. It is impossible to say what led the young man to follow his attacker, whom he had met earlier in a pub, to that particular spot, but it must be concluded from various ways he addressed and treated his potential victim that the attacker had assumed him to be gay. It is not clear what the student's response had been to his attacker's demands which were probably sexual, but finally he was beaten up and robbed. The details are not clear because the way the police handled the affair frightened the student into not wanting to press any charges for assault. Immediately after the incident he approached the police himself but probably realized, as they questioned him and told him why certain people go to that park at night, that others might think that he was homosexual, whereupon he quickly clammed up. My role in this was to stay with the student and to escort the police on council property, the regulations of which were totally ignored. I was brusquely told by the police to mind my own business. I already knew enough about the student and his background, favourite haunts, company and activities to make me think that underlying his relationship problems was a sexual identity problem, but all further counselling work with him after the police intervention in this case was quite fruitless. The student's work suffered greatly and before the end of the first year he was obliged to return home.

I did manage to speak to the police officers who dealt with the case. I agreed with them that the student should co-operate and press charges in view of the seriousness of the assault, but privately I held out no hope of this. In the course of the conversation they made it clear to me that the main reason they wanted to bring the attacker to book was not that he had carried out an assault which could also be deemed racist as the student was black, but because he was most likely to be a 'queer'. I don't suppose it occurred to either officer that in using this word they were actually addressing another queer. Needless to say I didn't tell them, nor anything about my previous conversations with the student. A lot of damage had been done and nothing could undo it by then. The police finally did get a conviction on the attacker, but for another offence. The student was again pressed to give testimony but he refused.

STEPHEN

A month ago two friends, Robin and Darren, were staying at my flat. Robin left the next morning having helped himself to $180 and a Walkman belonging to a guest of our landlord. A number of things influenced how Darren and I responded. One was the possibility of getting the stuff returned since Robin admitted the theft; another was the desire to avoid possible publicity – our landlord is a notable public figure and it would have been unfair to risk having him involved; and the third was the fact that an honest account of what had happened would have necessitated us all admitting our homosexuality, with potentially serious repercussions for Robin, since he was seventeen and sleeping with Darren, and any others who could subsequently be associated with Robin. Added to which, Robin's involvement with drugs meant that reporting what had happened to the police, however justified we felt, risked opening a can of worms of uncertain proportions. The point is, you see, that we cannot trust the police to be dispassionate and objective about our homosexuality, can we? It is a 'grave moral disorder' after all! We decided not to report the matter. Of course, Robin may well have assumed we wouldn't. In the end we retrieved only the Walkman.

I fear that the police, if they had investigated, would find out about my own offences: those of almost every gay man who has sex with anyone under the age of twenty-one, with more than one man at the same time or in a room which is not securely locked; the same person who cruises when he walks down Oxford Street and is prepared to kiss his friends in public. Is this paranoia? And if so does it not say as much about the state we live in as my interpretation of the role of police in it?

ARTHUR

A friend's lover, let's call him Barry, was attacked in October 1990 by neighbours in a housing estate where he had a council flat. Quite obviously, the attack was made because he is gay, there is no other known reason. He suffered a broken leg and many other injuries but, worst of all, he has lost part of a thumb. However, I understand that the physical injuries are insignificant compared with the total effect this has had on him. He is unable to work, unable to leave his flat unless someone else is with him. Worse still he is inclined to blame himself and to say that he is 'going to be straight from now on'.

Through the assistance of a housing association he was able to move away from the area where the attack occurred, but this has hardly helped because he just cannot face the outside world. Of course, his lover has done everything he can, including trying to arrange counselling, but so far Barry is still in shock after four months.

I asked whether the police had been brought in. They had, but they made no attempt to identify and charge any of the attackers. It seems that a day or two after the attack, Barry went out and hit one of his attackers. The police then charged *him* with assault. He was convicted, but given a suspended sentence. The judge expressed considerable curiosity as to why the police had not brought charges against the original assailants, but took it no further than that. Barry, I understand, is not prepared to lay charges, he would prefer to put the whole thing behind him. I am upset and angry. The young man has been forced into half believing that it is all his fault. I fear that other such things are happening all over the country. Recent reports from the Isle of Man may not be typical, but they indicate that extreme homophobia can still exert frightening power in this country and get away with it. It is easy to say that Barry should have gone straight to one of the civil liberties organizations as I would have done. I want to make the point that one needs to have a considerable political education to know how to defend oneself in the present climate of homophobia, to know where to seek help and to have the courage to carry it through.

CHARLES

My own personal experience with our boys in blue has, I regret to say, left me more than reticent ever to seek their assistance or advice. I have every good reason to mistrust their worthiness. Through a contact made on one of the nationwide gay phone-line links, I invited a young man to visit me after a correspondence of several months. We seemed to get along quite well, and he stayed overnight. However, after I had driven him to the station and returned home, I discovered, on tidying the room in which he had slept, that he had helped himself to a number of items from drawers in a chest which had contained valuable trinkets among other things. I knew instantly that they could only have been removed by him as he had been the only person in the room since I had last seen the missing items. I rang him later that evening but got no answer, whereupon I rang again early the following morning to be told that he no longer lived at that address and had left no forwarding address.

I decided to have a word with the local police and rang to make an appointment as I felt that I would prefer to talk to them in my home rather than at the station. I told them it was a robbery, hence I received a visit from the plain-clothes division. I explained the circumstances which led to my discovery and said that this had been the first time I had met the young man though I felt that I knew him after a lengthy exchange of letters. When I was asked how I came to know of him, I explained the contact through the gay line. The officer then changed his hitherto pleasant and attentive manner and asked me point blank if I was 'one of those'. I asked him to be more explicit and then he asked me was I 'bent'. I said that I was gay to which he replied, 'Well, sir, if you're one of that lot, what do you expect? They are all queer in more ways than one. If you invite a weirdo into your home, well, you know what I mean?' I was totally shattered by this and from that point he did not want to know anything more about the incident, only adding that he could not see anything the police could do. I suggested that this young man may be touring the country preying on and robbing other men and should there not be something done. He told me that in his opinion this poofter would never be caught and so long as he was moving around among his own lot there was no danger to the public. I was not a member of his public, I was 'one of them' and had to look out for myself.

I was once assaulted by a gang of queerbashers, being singled out while leaving a club one night. I staggered into the nearest police station to get help. On finding out that the assault had taken place outside a gay club they grilled me as to what had provoked the attack. Was I sure I had not offended the assailants, was I a homo, did I rent myself, did I drive there and if so had I been drinking, no words of comfort or any concern about my injuries. I could make a complaint if I wanted but they doubted if anything would come of it. I felt and was treated like a felon because I was 'one of them'. I have no faith or confidence in the police and, I fear, my experience has been compared to numerous similar such incidents involving friends of mine in this somewhat macho county area where I live.

PAUL

I have come to distrust the police in general and have adopted a policy of non-co-operation. Perhaps this stems initially from the fact that my father was a police officer and my relationship with him was far from sweet. I had opportunity to witness at firsthand the arrogance and violence directed at me and my mother by him, also the fact that most of his colleagues were on some 'fiddle' or other which they viewed as the perks of their job.

I was brought up to attend and worship in the Church of Scotland, inheriting a strong evangelical faith which led to a conversion and commitment experience of Christianity at the age of thirteen. Throughout my life I have maintained a strong belief in the God who is revealed – in His Son Jesus Christ, in the Bible and in the testimony of the Church. Therefore, my Christian commitment is much more than an intellectual assent to a revealed truth or moral code of behaviour, but is very much part of me as a person, affecting my reactions and outlook. By the age of nineteen I had been working in a Glasgow office for two years and I was actively involved in a pentecostal/evangelical church group. I began, too, at this time to be exercised in a public preaching and teaching ministry within the church, which led to me functioning as a full-time minister, latterly with a pentecostal church denomination. Formal training for the ministry was not considered important in the circles in which I was, so I did not complete any formal theological studies at college or university. However, as a voracious reader and Bible student and reading all kinds of literature, I gained a broader outlook than many of my fellows.

I first became aware of my homosexual orientation when I was twenty, but regarding it as a sin I sought to suppress it. Up until that time I had little contact with others of my own age group, my work in the ministry further isolating me since most church members were elderly. This may account for the late stage at which I fully realized my sexual orientation. My work with the church took me from Glasgow to Edinburgh and then to Wales. While there, at the age of twenty-two, I decided to wrestle, face up to and try to deal with the homosexual feelings which had plagued me. In an attempt to find a cure, I spent time in prayer, fasting, even repenting, such were the guilt feelings. During these times I realized that God accepted me as I was, and that at worse, if my homosexual feelings were a sin, then they were no greater or lesser than any other sin. This realization in itself was something of a breakthrough. Therefore, I followed the formula for relief of sin – confession, repentance and acceptance of forgiveness, which had proved effective for every other situation, yet my homosexual feelings remained. I concluded that these feelings were part of my nature; this again brought relief from the anxiety, distress and fear that I had experienced. I realized that perhaps for the first time I was accepting myself as I was, as God had made me, and as He accepted me. My next step in the ministry took me to London.

I should perhaps point out that I had never shared any of my feelings with any of my fellow Christians, and there was nothing in my speech or manner to betray me. Also I had never had any sexual relationship, either homosexual or heterosexual, so celibacy seemed to be my only course. However, in London I had more freedom and opportunity than in the small Welsh town that I had come from. Within a short time I discovered the 'gay scene' and formed a relationship with a fellow Christian. I had no difficulty concerning my public and private life, they were both kept in separate compartments as it were.

Difficulties came when I was posted back to Scotland to pioneer and attempt to revitalize a small elderly congregation in a town near Glasgow. I felt that this would mean an end to my homosexual activity and freedom which I had found in London. I soon found myself seeking out the 'gay scene' in Glasgow, and made contact with the Gay Christian Movement. I had returned to Scotland in May 1984. By August of the same year circumstances had occurred which were to change my experience dramatically. Returning to spend a few days in Glasgow one Sunday evening after church service, I was apprehended in the public conveniences at the bus station where I had arrived by two police officers and charged with committing a homosexual offence in a public place. At the time I protested and still maintain my innocence in spite of how events transpired. I was formally charged at the police station, photographed, fingerprinted and spent four hours in a cell before being released. During this time I had no fear or panic and remained calm throughout the ordeal. This was the beginning of a five-month nightmare and test of faith.

My initial reaction was to inform my superiors and tender my resignation, return to London and lose myself there. After consulting a clergyman friend from the Gay Christian Movement, I decided not to do this but to carry on as normal as an innocent person until such time as a summons might arrive. Nearly three months passed before a summons was delivered and I had a decision to make. I had to take the risk of there being some publicity, particularly in the press. I felt that I could not face this or any further strain from the situation, and feared for the effect this would have on my family and future. Therefore, I decided to plead guilty through my legal representative in an effort to deal with the matter as swiftly as possible. I knew that I would be unable to face an appearance in court, and knew that this would mean a recorded conviction. The day of the hearing passed without incident and I paid the £25 fine imposed by the court.

Two months later I was summoned by my superiors to learn that they had received notification of the charge against me from the procurator fiscal's office. Although not obliged to, the procurator fiscal may choose to inform an employer if an employee is guilty of an offence at his discretion. I was dismissed immediately and instructed to remove myself and my possessions and not return to the church or town. I was also told not to attend any of the churches in the denomination. At the time I was told there would be an internal church enquiry at headquarters. I provided as much information as possible. I have heard nothing further from them.

I received news from friends in London that they had been informed of my activities and my lack of co-operation with the church authorities, and naturally they were distressed. I immediately travelled to London and met with friends, some of whom accepted me and remain my friends, others who preferred to accept the version given by the church authorities. I also met with the leader of the London church who is president of the denomination. He wanted to know if at any time in any place I had homosexual feelings or experiences, so I came out to him and told him plainly how I felt. He asked me if I were 'sick, perverted or what' and that surely I could not believe that these feelings were natural. Understandably my statement that I felt homosexuality was an alternative form of expression upset him.

Six months after the hearing it transpired that my co-accused had entered a plea of not guilty and I was therefore summoned as a witness for the prosecution. Since I was for the first time under oath I confirmed that I was as innocent as the accused and that the story told by the police constables was fiction. This, of course, didn't endear me to the court and I felt a great deal of hostility. I had known from the outset that it would be my word against that of two police officers and that the magistrate was bound to agree with their opinion.

The fact and fear of a criminal conviction is still something that causes me occasional anxiety. I do not mind being known as a gay man but the criminal conviction and involvement with the police makes things much more sordid. Since I am now living with my lover I do not wish any involvement or contact with the police. Recently there was a house to house questioning concerning a murder locally. While I was willing to give basic facts the knowledge that when my name was fed into their computer this conviction would appear did frighten me – irrationally of course, but then most fears are irrational.

I do have a concern for the many who have a conflict and are suffering under condemnation because of their sexual orientation and religious commitment. It is my hope that in some small way through my experience that others might find hope and faith in Christ whatever their sexual orientation and be set free with the liberty that He alone brings.

PETER

I was in Brighton in September 1990, a few days after a gay barman had been robbed and murdered. The police were questioning everyone in the gay bar I was in. As I had arrived in Brighton after the murder they asked if I had been there during the previous three months, which I confirmed. I was shown two photographs and they took my name, but I would not give them my address or the name of my home town. Later, I told other men who were commending the police for their vigilance that they were compiling a list of homosexuals for 'when the holocaust comes'. They apparently always do this when a gay murder occurs and even asked a friend of mine in a case in Bristol to give them a list of his friends so that they could be eliminated. He refused. I shall use a false name if it happens to me again. I wasn't being merely cynical about the reasons for making these lists. The murderer has still not been found. Are the lists still in existence? If so, for whose benefit?

Section 28 of the Local Government Act, 1988, which proscribed the 'promotion of homosexuality' and 'pretended families' in schools and in local government-funded projects and events, when still Clause 28, galvanized the lesbian and gay community into action and protest in an entirely unprecedented way. Three years later, Clause 25 of the Criminal Justice Bill sought to stiffen the penalties for several crimes with which gay men are frequently charged and was seen as the precursor to a possible recriminalization of male homosexuality. At the end of 1990 an Old Bailey judge sentenced eight men to up to four and a half years in prison for consensual S/M sex sessions and related offences.

RICHARD

The following are excerpts from my diary over the last five months concerning the Clause:

'The lobby was great. At least eight hundred attended, getting on for a thousand all told. The visitors rather looked down on the rampant socializing of the London lot, but it's natural when you spend a cold afternoon in line with a load of friends. I think Corbyn, the Labour MP, was quite impressed. This could be important. Ever since the end of the Gay Liberation Front there's been a need for gay politics without offputting sectarian radicalism or the gentle do-gooding liberalism of CHE. I think that as OLGA faces a real crisis it might be the focus of something important. There's nothing like a threat to bring people together. . . .

'I'm really depressed by the clause, which looks like the beginning of the end and just what I've been fearing and expecting since I first heard about AIDS. Not that there's a simple cause and effect relationship by any means. The tide certainly is turning and I'm amazed how many people still don't realize. The fact is many, most, gay men and lesbians lead quietly ghettoized lives, out to close friends and sometimes colleagues but with no conception of sexual politics. Having lived among out and politicized people, I'm only just getting an impression of the extent of complacency and disinterest that exists among gay people. I felt this particularly strongly on Friday night at the Bull and Pump and waiting for coffee at Gay's The Word today after a morning of heavy shopping. Gill asked the guy ahead of me if he was going to the lobby. He said he might if he was told where and when. I made a slight scene about how important it was. Probably less effective than her gentle prod. . . .

'There were twelve thousand five hundred reckoned to be on the march and the stewarding was quite difficult, though everything was hassle-free until we got to Whitehall. Just ahead of me a group crossed the road and started shouting by the Downing Street railings. The stewards all ran there and it got very ugly, with the police pushing people back, the rest of the march pushing us on from behind and each surge resulting in a couple being taken out by the police and arrested in the empty space behind them. There was no way it could end; it carried on until the start of the march had been got going again. I was actually frightened

– the tell-tale nervous tic in my right leg – and while the damage to the peaceful demonstration is regrettable I too feel the frustration that fuels anger, only with me it never does that. It's so simple to blame people, but so cowardly not to. The march continued to a dreary park by the Imperial War Museum. Robyn Tyler gave a great speech that moved me to tears. She is very funny – "You know Ronald Reagan? He's Margaret Thatcher in drag." . . . "If it wasn't for Michelangelo the Sistine Chapel would be covered in wallpaper." . . . "Anita Bryant is to religion what painting by numbers is to art." . . . "This guy said, 'I think there should be an island where all the sexual deviants are put together.' I said, 'There is dear. It's called England.' " – and very passionate about how what we are defending is love. . . .

'Everyone was there. Gill's friend of the same age reminisced about lobbying in a group in double figures in 1965. He thought it was great that so many people could join in a demo like this one and that there was no going back. I have great admiration for the courage of people like him but don't agree. How many people *should* have been on the streets today? Tens of thousands. I didn't dare go out this evening because I would have felt bitter at the Complacent. I do. And I know that this feeling is a waste of my energies. Went home for a bath. Nothing on Thames News. The greatest bias of the press is the power of silence. . . .

'The police picked people off for kissing, offensive weapons such as banners and so on, on the way out of the park, at least thirty-five arrests altogether. The vigil this evening outside the Cannon Row police station was a mistake in practice as there was only one person held there and fourteen at Kennington. But it was essentially symbolic. In practice, we were impotent, the police would not say what the man had been charged with and when we were moved back and one person was taken in they wouldn't even release his name and wouldn't let us see either of them. The first man's friend was not told that he could give surety at his local police station so got a taxi in. We waited from six to almost nine and he was let out, as was the other guy. This latter wouldn't have happened if we hadn't stayed. The release at nine amounted to a sort of climax for the evening. In spite of the rain we sang spiritedly. Only three of us, me being one, knew all the words of 'I Am What I Am', though when the other two went on to *Follies* and *Oz* I was comforted by the fact that they were a good six years younger than me.

'This evening it was the Clause 27 meeting. Interesting to contrast what the meeting was – bickering between gays and straights, calls for caucuses by blacks, and arguments over something called "structure" – "We must get the structure right" – whereas the Arts Lobby has arranged a press conference, two flyposter campaigns, a slot on Channel Four, an exclusive interview by using Billy Bragg and Ian McKellen and a general mailing. Arts organizations needs must have a flair for cheap and instant publicity. The Association of London Authorities has a good briefing package on the Lords, and is already looking beyond the Bill as it must while the campaign is arguing over whether to rename itself, as Clause 27 is now Clause 28. Last night it was an abortive Tower Hamlets meeting. The Arts Lobby meeting this afternoon was quite successful. I started feeling very depressed at the effect of the Bill as we all rehearsed its consequences for us, though I was the only one to state its importance as the first attempt to control the creative agenda by legislation. The good things were seeing lesbians and gay men fighting for a common cause, an absence of party politics, so different to my Union campaigning days, and everyone asking, "What can *I* do?". . . .

'Midnight, Tuesday. I have just heard on the radio that Clause 28 has been approved by the Lords. *Today in Parliament* stated that their Lordships then went on to discuss Clause 29, the repeal of the dog licence, about which there was a rather more vigorous and informed debate. What, I ask myself, is the point in any campaign now? Certainly not to change the minds of the Commons. It will happen, and we all know that. To express anger and indignation? To what end? Surely we should be developing ways of fighting it the way the ALA is doing, redesigning job descriptions, preparing fighting funds. All I know is that the next demo is going to be bigger and angrier. And the worst of it is that those who sat on their backsides and didn't do a thing have, for that very reason, proved themselves right. Was there really any chance of anything else happening? I really thought so. I actually believed in an element of human rationality, though I've so often preached the opposite: go on, burn, destroy, riot, there's no need for you to respect the laws of the land, 'cos they sure as hell don't respect you.'

The campaign has had positive features. I recall one evening being in a bookshop in Charing Cross Road where the radio was playing *Third Ear*, a Radio 3 arts discussion programme which was considering the Clause, with Peregrine Worsthorne and Ian McKellen I think. When the programme ended the clientele of the bookshop spontaneously started extending the discussion in a way I've never seen before in this country. And we were by no means all opposed to the Clause or all for the same reasons.

Although gay men and lesbians are for the first time threatened together and fighting together I have seen a lot of bickering that has left me disillusioned and burned out. No, this isn't our Stonewall, though that may come out of it. Stonewall was a single symbolic event that crystallized resentments, frustrations and angers. A political campaign can't do that. I don't think violence does any good though I'm beginning to wonder what will. Under the present government there is no point in trying to reverse the law. I think legal defence and test cases and going to the European Court is the best thing to do until we get rid of the present administration.

JAMES

At the time Section 28 was introduced, the government and media were actively engaged in whipping up a climate of hatred against gays. I have no doubt that sections of the Tory party and its supporters were genuinely convinced that they were right to 'do something about the family' and, equally genuinely, saw Section 28 as a legitimate way of doing it which, they could claim, did not compromise the individual's right to free expression. They say 'promotion of homosexuality' as an instance of gays' freedom of expression (ho ho, what 'freedom'?) interfering with the freedom of heterosexuals to reproduce themselves and their heterosexuality.

We are now slightly post-Thatcher. The climate is slightly less harsh. These days the government seems to me to be less committed, perhaps it feels there is less necessity, to banging the drum of heterosexism. It has arguably withdrawn some of the reasoning behind Section 28 that it originally supported so vociferously. This retreat had begun to happen quite soon after the introduction of the Local Government Bill, for instance when it was realized that most of the legislation concerning sex education had already been adequately dealt with in the Education Acts and that it is school governors, and not local authorities, who are principally responsible for the nature and character of this.

Nevertheless the right-wing media remain as determined as ever to wipe gays off the map. They continue to highlight the speeches of loony right MPs and to give column room to the likes of Gary Bushell to whip up and keep homophobia on the boil.

There *was* cause for alarm about Section 28 and there still *is*. I have not personally been affected by it, though I have become aware of its effect in arts funding by local authorities in some cases. One could argue that it is sleeping and that we could ignore it. Alternatively, it is quite conceivable that, like some of the customs legislation, it might, a hundred years from now, be dusted down and pressed into service in some oppressive way. So, though I am still very cynical about what is possible in the peculiar British sexual climate, I suppose we must continue to campaign against it until it, and *all* legislation like it, is permanently removed from the statute books.

For the same reason, Clause 25 of the Criminal Justice Bill should now be resisted. This is further evidence of the determination of a tendency within the Tory party which knows it can rely on the sort of mindless jingoistic support of *Sun*-reading proles to persecute gays because their lifestyle does not accord with what they perceive as morally acceptable. There is little chance of reason prevailing in such a climate. The sort of people who are drafting this legislation in that form are the same bigoted, moronic, ideological philistines who drafted the first lot. The only difference between them and the *Sun*-reading proles is that the former have slightly posher accents. They simply don't have the intellectual capacity to realize that the instances they are lumping together in one clause are anything but of a single piece.

I was horrified, but not altogether surprised, by the judgment of Judge James Rant in the case of the S/M fourteen. The men concerned will appeal. It's possible that the sentences might be reduced but they will have great difficulty arguing that they have been involved in 'victimless crimes'. The British attitude to sex and sexuality simply does not allow of such fine distinctions. We live in a society in which people are not encouraged even to reflect on the values involved in such matters. Intellect must not be applied in this area. The only distinctions to be made are as follows:

1 All heterosexual missionary activity by officially married persons is 'love', i.e. *good*.
2 Heterosexual missionary activity by unmarried persons is
'bonking', i.e. *OK*.
3 Anything else, ranging from kinky to perverted is 'sex', i.e.
bad.

The function of (1) which of course includes marital rape and
father–daughter incest is to bolster people's feelings of normalcy
and perpetuate the heterosexist system of self- and other-
oppression.

The function of (2) is to provide occasional relief from (1)
which, though few would be prepared to admit it, would otherwise be too boring.

The function of (3) is to increase newspaper profits.

The converse of this view is that the value of a person's 'chosen
way of life', from the perspective of Tory legislators and *Sun*
readers, is measured in terms of what they do with their own
and others' 'naughty bits'. If a couple fucks like rabbits fuck (i.e.
without sensibility, intellectualization, sensitivity, emotionality,
consideration, reflection, memory or imagination) they probably
already have between them all the requisite qualifications to
become adequate parents (i.e. a male naughty bit, a female
naughty bit and a male orgasm). Conception and parenthood
result. End of story. If conception is missing, adoption may be
recommended provided the rabbit-like devotion to marital duties
persists.

Bucks who fuck other does, or, heaven forbid, does who fuck
other bucks, are considered to be exercising too much imagination. Even if they are doing it in order to become parents, it
still counts as either bonking or sex and is thus impermissible.
In this I have probably been extremely unfair to rabbits.

In referring back to what I wrote at the time of Section 28 the
reader will be aware that my cynicism in such matters remains
undimmed! Then, I wrote: 'I think the impetus for the necessary
political change in Britain will not come from within the present
political arena with its withered range of demoralized and stulti-
fied yes-persons, their egomaniacal perspectives and utterly inef-
fectual pretence at opposition, but from beyond our shores
altogether. Most of the UK's gays and lesbians will not only
have come out but gone out and emigrated, together with their

pretended families and their homosexual PR agencies, to Norway, Denmark or East Germany, anywhere where the other nine-tenths of humanity are prepared to speak their language.

'Having conducted the affairs of parliament for a further thirty years from Dulwich by means of levers and strings connected to her faithful acolytes, Thatcher will have retired to her deathbed, protesting her infallibility to the last. The Great Straight British Public, cowed into total subservience to the moral standards of James Anderton by a combination of the Official Secrets Act 1989, 1990 and 1991, and the introduction of a national system of specialized cesspits in which to swirl degenerates, will be shielded from the awful knowledge that SHE has actually passed on, and will continue to read the *Sun*, which will have eclipsed every other publication by then, marry, sexually abuse their children, flail themselves, mass murder each other for fun and dye their hair blue for a further fifty years.

'Meanwhile, South Africa will be non-racial, the Soviet Union will be Green and a decentralized China will be efficiently governed by eight-year-olds. And slowly, ever so, ever so slowly the great-grandchildren and great-great-grandchildren of the imbeciles who voted for Thatcherism will remove the paper-bags from their heads and, if their hearing is still intact, may well be deafened by the laughter of the rest of the world.'

DAVID

In all the debate, although little logic prevailed, over Section 28, I have not heard the answers to these questions:

1 What is so inherently disappointing about heterosexuality that people will turn lesbian or gay if given the slightest opportunity?
2 What is so inherently exciting about homosexuality that people, given the option, would prefer it?
3 What is it about the teaching of sexuality that suddenly makes a teacher superb, able to sway a whole class in a few lessons towards whatever viewpoint is expressed, whereas in most other subjects this is impossible?

Heterosexual propaganda is overwhelming. Some of the advocates of Clause 28 suggest that homosexuality is increasing under the influence of 'homosexual propaganda' yet fail to realize that, as society's attitudes have changed, so it has become easier to live openly as gay and be accepted as such. The increasing numbers of people being honest and open about their sexuality should not be confused with an increase in the frequency of people who prefer their own gender.

I attended both the anti-clause demo and Pride '88 and have never before felt such a sense of community with other people. Maybe this was a pretend family; I like it anyway. One of the most memorable speeches of the two days was made by Lord Falkland, a peer who had become involved in the anti-clause movement because he feared censorship in the arts. He explained how, as a straight man, he had become involved in the anti-clause movement from one perspective alone, but when he met so many gay men and lesbians who told him about their lives he then saw all of Clause 28 as threatening and insulting and was fully committed to fighting it all the way. In ending he stated that the best way to fight Clause 28 was not to go on marches or sign petitions, though these helped, but to go home and talk to people, lots of people, tell them about our lives and get them to join in. In the final analysis I believe that is the way to win, despite our being a minority. Lesbians and gay men have reason and logic on their side. We occupy what Mrs Thatcher calls 'the moral high ground' and, in the end, reason and logic must prevail over ignorance and bigotry.

Even as I write these words my spine tingles at the memory of fifty thousand people in Kennington Park singing at the tops of their voices, Tom Robinson's 'Glad to be Gay'.

What a day that was. . . .

3

Becoming

CLIVE

My first homosexual experience, although strictly speaking it can't really be defined as such as it was about the age of nine or ten and therefore before I became a 'sexual being', was one very hot summer night when I was spending the night with my cousin. He was a very good-looking boy; I had always had a crush on him. We were sleeping the night in a double bed and decided to strip naked to cool off. I guess that I was sexually aroused too, we both had erections. We spent a while just lying there admiring each other's body. We wrestled with each other, the evening culminating with each of us giving the other a piggy-back! In all this innocent fun I knew that I was 'different', but did not define myself as homosexual.

From about the age of eighteen I had bought magazines depicting naked men and had used them for masturbation. These were usually the *Health and Efficiency* magazine which was available quite openly. I used to save past issues and even cut out the better-looking young men to masturbate over. I used to have occasional pangs of guilt and disgust, however, and every so often I would dispose of or ritually burn my copies. My feelings used to come in spurts, often with intervals of weeks or months before my 'urge' started again. At the time of my getting over my emotions towards my own sex, I felt no regret at disposing of several pounds worth of magazines. I believed that I was 'getting the better' of my tendencies. It was only when the months of no feelings reduced to weeks and then to days with eventually a constant urge to satisfy myself that I began to do something about it.

By that time I had been married for nine-and-a-half years and all this had been going on behind my wife's back, I had said nothing to her and she had no idea of my difference from other men. I was twenty-nine, with a wife and two young children and very happy, but my sexual life, although never very good, was getting worse. I could not even achieve an erection for my wife on occasions, but could reach orgasm by myself in front of my pictures and with enough fantasizing. I thought I must do something about myself if I was to avoid the possibility of ruining my life. I was at university at that time and coming up to taking my first year's examinations and I was worried that I might flop them unless I spoke to someone about myself.

One Thursday night in May 1984, when my wife was out, I decided that I had better contact one of the two gay helplines. It was the first time that I had used the word homosexual to describe myself. The person at the other end was really helpful, he didn't laugh at me or think me queer. I was pleased to have spoken to someone and was even more pleased when he agreed to meet me for a discussion over a drink the following Monday. I could hardly wait till then, but Monday came along and I met him in a straight pub before I plucked up enough courage to go down to our one and only gay pub in the centre of the city with him. I was extremely nervous at the thought of what I might see, excited but apprehensive. Can you imagine the delight when upon entering the pub I found all the men inside to look just like me? There was no one in a dress, none wearing make-up and none carrying a handbag! You can understand the relief to me at discovering my real identity and it was nothing like those depicted in the media. I had found myself!

Back at his flat the counsellor showed me past copies of *Him* and the pictures of the good-looking models within, each with an erection – I had never seen a picture of a man with a hard-on – I got very aroused and so did he and the inevitable happened. We ended up in bed together. It was not particularly good, I just lay there as I didn't know what was expected of me, so I left it up to him to show me. I was not at all attracted to him, but the actual act of lying with a man turned me on. Afterwards though I was rather repulsed by it: the idea of doing something behind my wife's back, in secret, behind locked doors, unbeknown to his lover; and, strangely, the amount of mess gay sex could physically cause, the mopping up of double the quantity of semen afterwards, that I began to have doubts about myself and where

I was going. I did, however, allow myself to go with him the following week to a gay disco, just to see what it was all about. I was rather disappointed. My expectations were over the top. My hopes of seeing scantily clad young men in all sorts of erotic poses were all dashed. The evening turned out to be a bit of a washout, so much so that I refrained from going out on the gay scene again for another ten months.

I still had my feelings, they were just as strong as ever. I was still married, but our sex life was just as bad as ever, so again I decided to do something. On this occasion, in February 1985, I rang the other counselling helpline in the city and arranged to meet a married man working for them. I met him, we talked hard and that night I decided to tell my wife. All the next day I debated what I was to tell her, rehearsed it but it came out well enough, we had a few tears, but altogether she took it really well. When I came out to my mother she took it very well. She is very understanding and has even suggested to me that my father himself had, as a twenty-two-year-old soldier, a homosexual relationship.

I have achieved a high level of dignity with a strong identity, knowing that people accept me for what I really am rather than the act I was putting on before.

FRED

I was, from childhood to my late teens, very solitary. I was introverted, artistic, quiet and happy with my own company and it was only from fifteen onwards that I wondered why there didn't seem to be someone for me. I was overweight, wore glasses and was not the then conventional image. In fact I came to believe that fat people were ugly and ugly people were not loved. This idea has lasted for a great deal of my life and so precluded much interaction on a deep emotional level with anyone.

I was thirty-six when I came out to myself while actively caring for my mother who had had a stroke. She was sitting in her wheelchair dozing after lunch. I was washing up in the kitchen and, as has happened with other major life impulses previously, such was the force of the acknowledgement that I said out loud, 'You're gay!' I immediately checked that Mother was still dozing, she was, and I continued working and thinking. My initial reaction was that nothing would or could change. I continued to think this for about two weeks and then I realized that, while in the short term, or however long my caring situation would last, nothing would change, in the long term it would. I was trapped by the situation at home with no chance of being able to explore what being gay meant to me. There was an enormous sense of relief, a feeling that at last I was wearing the correct clothes and they fitted. It made complete and utter sense of who I was and what I'd done and hadn't done with my life up to that point. It all came at a time when 95 per cent of my life was directed towards caring for my mother, looking after us both, adopting, not for the first time, the 'female' role as perceived by the outside community, but simply doing something that needed doing. My mother and I had a very special relationship – I know it's the classic gay cliché, but we were best friends as well, telepathic to a degree that outsiders, including the family, found alarming and strange, but which we found completely normal.

I came out to two older friends at church – I am a spiritualist – and they were very open and supportive. Later, when my mother was in full-time hospital care I told my 'adopted' family whose reactions were, 'We've known that for years.' I was selective at first about who I told. I suppose I needed the support and acceptance of those I thought would help me by accepting me. Later, I met a man and we had a relationship which lasted six years. There were problems which resulted in separations. These unhappy periods led to my 'blood' family becoming aware of my situation. They came, reluctantly at first, to accept the fact through the good offices of my sister-in-law. Their acceptance is now total as they saw that I was not interested in the generally perceived stereotyped gay lifestyle, whatever that is. In fact, we have all become much closer because I have gradually forced them to accept me being very physical with them. As a family we were never demonstrative, now we all agree it was something we wanted to be. This gradual opening-out process also happened at work, a small building company. Most of the work-force had known me for a considerable time and accept the situation, even to the point of asking questions about various aspects and not the usual ones about what happens in bed, and who is the man and who the woman!

Gradually, especially after the break-up of the relationship, I found that to be secretive to some people and public with others is just too hard for me to maintain, so I'm out to everyone although I do live reasonably quietly, as I always did, but I will not refuse to acknowledge my gay persona. I have also become more political and the strength gained from the solidarity of taking part in a march, a meeting or a vigil, not to mention Scottish Pride in Edinburgh and, one week later, Pride '91 in London. They were incredible.

ARTHUR

In the working-class town in New Zealand where I lived until I was ten, the boys talked a great deal about male to male sex. It was more often laughed about than condemned. When I was nine, a cousin aged thirteen suggested that we try it, and I willingly agreed. He fucked me and I enjoyed it. We continued having sex together, though not frequently, until I was sixteen. I went to university young, at sixteen, and very soon had other partners and this continued, mostly with the same men, until I was twenty-five.

I did not, however, think of myself as homosexual. The people I knew mostly did not label themselves, and of course the word gay was never used. This was the 1940s. One friend was an exception. A few years older than me, with a lot of experience, he said he knew he would only ever be interested in men. He would sometimes exclaim, 'Toujours gai.' He was exceptionally daring in the places and occasions he would have sex. Everyone knew, but he was very well liked for his acting, singing and capacity to entertain.

At university I found references to homosexuality in books. I read English literature, and soon knew about Wilde and the ancient Greeks. On my parents' bookshelves I found a book called *There's a Porpoise Close Behind Us*, about gay life in the theatre in London in the 1920s. I think the author was Noel Langley. My stepmother told me not to read it, so of course I did. My friends and I heard rumours about Noël Coward.

So my perceptions were confused, and remained confused for a very long time. I enjoyed sex with men, especially with two of my partners, but when I was not with them I partly despised them, and even joined in, sometimes, in the abusive comments of other people.

As we moved into the 1950s the situation became worse. In

1947 I decided to accept the theory that my homosexuality was a phase and decided to be straight. My decision was partly concern about my career as a secondary-school teacher and partly fear of illegal behaviour. I had, by this time, moved to London. The 1950s saw many famous trials. The case of Alan Turing was particularly distressing, both the way he was made to take anti-sex-drive drugs and the way he had been convicted of a 'crime' in which the 'victim' was a very willing partner. I did not know the full story until I read Andrew Hodges' biography thirty years later.

I decided that it was up to the individual to *choose* his own sexuality. Also I wanted a settled way of life and I wanted children. Fear was more significant than guilt, though that was also important. The attempt at 'conversion' appeared to be successful, though there were three occasions in ten years when I had sex with men. After moderately satisfactory sexual relationships with four women, I married one of them in 1962. This marriage lasted in law for twenty-five years, and in bed for nearly twenty. But I knew after less than ten years of marriage that I was much more powerfully attracted to men.

The Sexual Offences Act in 1967 made a great difference to my feelings about my own homosexuality. I soon acknowledged to myself that I wanted to have sex with men. It has taken me another twenty years for me to get rid of the guilt I felt about it.

Nine years ago a friend from my student days reappeared and we had sex together. I decided it was time to look, actively, for a male lover. For a time my wife thought, and I agreed with her, that we could still live together, but four years ago she said we should divorce and I agreed. We have, in fact, a judicial separation rather than a divorce, to protect her right to a widow's pension from my superannuation. We meet amicably from time to time. She has met my lover and shows no hostility. My daughter, aged twenty-six, and my son of twenty-four have happily accepted my being gay. They meet my lover frequently and like him. My son is at university and lives with me when he is not away at college. He has a lover of the opposite sex. My daughter is a tenant in a flat in the same house as me. She has a same-sex lover. This is quite recent and she is very happy about it, but has not yet decided whether she wants to describe herself as lesbian.

I have never discussed my sexuality with my father. My mother died when I was an infant. My stepmother, with whom I have always been on excellent terms, must have heard about what I was doing with male friends when I was seventeen. She said, 'If you really are attracted more to men, you ought not to pretend you are not.' That was a fairly remarkable position to take up in 1940. However, I denied it strongly and she never raised the subject again. She is now ninety, and next year she will meet my lover in New Zealand. She has said in advance that she is looking forward to meeting him, and I feel confident that they will get on well together.

CLIFF

My first contact with the homosexual world came about by accident when I was nearing my twentieth birthday. Prior to this I cannot recall ever feeling any inclinations towards members of my own sex; not even during adolescence. I'd had a couple of steady girlfriends and was on the verge of becoming engaged to a girl that I had been going out with for over two years.

This first contact happened when I was taken to a gay nightclub by a lad I had known at school. I was very drunk. That was not unusual in those days as I knocked around with the local motorbike gang. When I heard he was going nightclubbing I pleaded with him to take me along. It was then he told me he was going to a gay club, and that he thought I'd hate it and probably cause trouble if I went.

To cut a long story short, I did go and thoroughly, if warily, enjoyed myself. I was invited by a young man to go back to his flat after the club for a drink. Never one to refuse a drink I agreed, knowing I could take care of myself if he tried anything on with me. Back at his flat he handed me a drink and, sure enough, sat down next to me. He gave me a pile of gay porno magazines to read. It was the first time I'd seen such things. I looked through them, he had his hand on my leg and I was bored to tears. If this is gay life, I thought, it's not for me. Too boring. So I very impolitely left.

This seemingly innocuous occurrence was, however, to change my entire life. I started visiting the local gay bar and club regularly, on my own. I didn't get off with anyone and didn't particularly want to. When I did first have sex with a man it seemed to me to be just as natural as sex with a girl. I enjoyed a relation-ship with this man for many months. To me he was a good, easy screw; to him I was the one he loved. It took me many months to understand how a man can love another man, or a woman another woman.

Things at home started to change drastically. Although I'd never hidden the fact that I went to gay bars and often spent the night at my parents' house with my lover, my mother never really approved, though my father did. I broke off, with relief, my relationship with my girlfriend of whom my father never approved. Soon, though, my father died and my mother and brother literally threw me out onto the streets because I'm gay. They still don't speak to me after five years.

Having to fend for myself for the first time, having little money and nowhere to live plunged me into depression. However, I had many friends and they rallied round to help me. I found a place to live and, through the kindness of a very good straight friend who gave me a copy of James Baldwin's *Giovanni's Room* for me to read, I grew to understand about homosexual love.

EDWARD

I soon got into the clubbing period of my life. I would go out with a group of male friends, get drunk and finish the evening by trying to have the last slow dance with a bird. I hated this meat market but continued with the game as it was expected of me. I would still ask someone to dance at the end of the evening, but as soon as the record finished I would politely say thank you and move away without making any chat-up attempt. I told myself that the lack of interest was due to the fact that I didn't know the person I was dancing with. I would not ask out women I knew because I wanted to avoid the awkwardness and the embarrassment a refusal would bring. Why the women them-selves would consent to dance with such a bunch of loud and boisterous piss artists in the first place, however, is still beyond me. I suppose that they were under similar social pressures.

By the time I was twenty I had made it quite impossible for me to attempt any sexual or deep emotional contact with anyone. In fact, the thought of sex left me cold. The thought of being gay did not even enter my head.

In 1985 I started working for a company which was comprised

of many small units situated in a small area. The people I worked with were around my age and I got to know the people working in my unit and the other units quite well. I became quite attached to another male colleague without seeing any significance. There were openly gay workers in some of the other units, two of whom fascinated me during my first Christmas party at the firm. The older one was wearing a pink teddy bear key-ring improvised into an earring and was sitting with the younger guy on his knee. This was my first positive image of homosexuality. I found myself watching them whenever either had to come into my unit for any reason. One of them would sometimes invite the straight members of my unit to Heaven, but I was never asked which upset me a bit as I was dying to find out what it was all about – for purely academic reasons, of course. . . . These people became an obsession with me, but, obviously misreading my fascination and discomfort as homophobia, they would not let me be on any social speaking terms with them.

I left that job by 1986 and over the next couple of years I became very interested in the homosexual phenomenon. I would watch any positive film on the television, many of which were safe American films where the gays were sexless. I first began to question my sexuality when I saw *My Beautiful Laundrette*. I watched the love scene in the back of the laundrette and was thunderstruck. Not only were two men kissing on the telly, they were doing it very passionately. My breathing and heartbeat quickened and at last I noticed my sexuality running and screaming into consciousness.

These feelings were reinforced when I took a lift home one night in a stranger's car. (Didn't my mother ever warn me?) I worked part-time in a bar at weekends and after a club night I found myself waiting for a night bus at three o'clock in the morning. A car pulled up and the middle-aged driver asked me the time. I told him. He then asked me where I was going and offered to give me a lift. Being very naive and still having thirty minutes to wait for my bus, I accepted. He got on to the subject of sex and decided that deep down I was really a latent homosexual. We had a long chat about it. When he dropped me off he had not convinced me to let him masturbate me, but he had succeeded in making me take my would-be sexuality more seriously.

In July 1987 I met someone from the bar in which I work and

I have lived with him for the last two years. When my mother heard about him she decided not to like him, possibly because this was the final proof that I would not get married. When she did meet him she found this impossible, and found him quite charming. When I visit my father my sexuality is not mentioned. I am trying to win him round subtly and slowly but I have heard that he and my sister-in-law had a big row over me where he blamed my lover for my being gay and she warned him that if he forced me to choose between him and my lover he will probably lose.

I started telling people that I was bisexual to ease the shock. This was not a good idea as some people took this to mean that I would eventually grow out of this phase and become 'normal'. The first person I told was an old school friend. He simply said, 'Good, I'm for any form of perversion!' People tend to say that they thought I was straight, which is annoying as a few years ago, when I thought I was straight, people used to ask me if I was gay. I'll never understand people.

LESLIE

I never remember seeing or hearing anything positive about same-sex relationships, and could not bring myself to admit that that was what I needed until I was twenty-six. My teens and early twenties were therefore a horribly lonely, confused time. My trouble was associating the love and attraction I felt for men with the unpleasant reputation surrounding homosexuality. I could never link the two. It was not until, some years after moving away from my parents and being in my own flat, first a woman and then a young man invited themselves into my bed (I would never have had the courage to make the first move) that things began to fall into place. Sleeping and having sex with him was much more exciting and satisfying than doing it with her. She made me feel guilty for not getting turned on.

At the time I was taking LSD, and during a deliberate trip back into my memory I became certain that whatever it was in me that made me gay had been there all the time, and could never go away. So, at long last, I told myself that I was gay. After that it was surprisingly easy really, apart from my chronic shyness. Although in some ways I feel I wasted my youth, in others I think that the wait until my mid-twenties meant that I was able to handle coming out fairly painlessly. And as one who still doesn't care for the pubs and clubs there wasn't much for me to come out to until around the time I did.

PAT

Growing up in Northern Ireland immediately after the Second World War in a family which was desperately poor was very difficult. Survival was the only game and, I think, because of my father's illness and my mother's silence, I quickly learned to live inside myself while being good at giving the outside world due recognition. There is no doubt, at every turn, for many years, and even today when thirty-nine cases of men in public lavatories are causing scandal, suicide and breakdown, Northern Ireland's attitudes to gays is hostile, sometimes fiercely so. The images of homosexuals presented were always of vile, sick people who couldn't be trusted, were bitchy, camp, unhappy and not in any sense normal.

I think, recently, I've begun to see and accept myself positively, and I've met a number of people who are confident, articulate and glad to be gay. It has taken me nearly three years of counselling to get to the point where I'm glad to be me. A lot of that, sure, is related to being gay but then a lot isn't, and that is as positive as it was when I pretended, as I did, for nearly forty plus years that I wasn't. However, having come out to my wife and a number of close friends, there is a marked tendency for them to see me only in a gay context as if the other abilities I had have disappeared or have become devalued or tainted.

There have been examples of great love and courage which have helped. Recently a close friend had a lover who died of AIDS and he, my friend, never left his bedside for the last forty-eight hours, or his room for the preceding month. That's immense love by any standards and it can't be made impure because it's two men. Another friend, a policeman, was found *in flagrante delicto* in his car with a friend. When the papers got to hear of it they had a field day. He had to tell his parents and his mother cried loudly that she'd rather he had been killed by a bomb. His father still doesn't refer to him or use his name even when at dinner. To stay there and be with them given that level of non-verbal violence demands great courage and, again, that can't be worthless and vile.

Seventeen years of marriage have meant that my disguise was well nigh perfect. During the last ten years I've talked a lot to three male friends. I've talked, they've listened. They were all contemporaries of mine, tolerant, totally confidential and totally straight. There was no judgement, only acceptance of me and sympathy for my pain and despair. They didn't try to alter me or hinder me, they did remind me forcefully of the dangers of cottaging and of being with rentboys in London, for my own, my wife's and my children's sake. Others I've told have talked about sustained celibacy to save the marriage, likening being gay to some sort of physical disability like from a road accident which paralyses you from the waist down. I don't feel paralysed and I don't feel ill. I just want to be with, touch and make love to other men. At no time did I think of a 'cure'. I thought of a terminus, a hundred paracetamols and a bottle of brandy. And I've thought of injecting mercury. But I don't think being gay is wrong. It causes me intense pain, loneliness and despair but it's not wrong.

EUGENE

I first had sex with another man when I was twenty-five. He was a prostitute I picked up one Saturday afternoon in one of the main cruising areas in Dublin. I didn't have a car so we went to the toilet of a nearby pub. I remember the customers were downstairs so we could hear the sound of Saturday afternoon racing on the TV. When the coast was clear we locked ourselves in the toilet and he sucked me off. It was a strange experience and I remember I felt guilty afterwards, not in religious terms, but at exploiting him. I think I paid him £20.

I didn't have sex after that for another three years. I was still very firmly in the closet and stayed in not out of any sense of shame but basically because Dublin is such a small place and I was worried that my parents would find out. I had never gone to the gay pubs or clubs and now I very much regret that I wasted all of my twenties. Only in 1989 when I was approaching thirty did I start to get active in any sort of consistent way. Firstly it was by picking up prostitutes and taking them either to my flat or else bringing them to the beach or an open park in the middle of the night. Mostly they were boys in their early twenties. After years of celibacy the release was wonderful. I enjoyed the cruising for the boys as much as the sex itself. Frequently I had them dress up in jeans, Doc Martens boots, donkey or leather jackets before beginning sex. It was a liberation.

Two of the men I met in these encounters were not prostitutes but were other punters like me. One took me home to his house and we went to bed together. We had sex and talked for a long time. I left about 3 am. It was the first time I had been to bed, literally, with another man. The second has become a good friend. He introduced me to the scene in Dublin and I will always be grateful to him for that act of kindness.

In 1990 I first went to the London Lesbian and Gay Centre. This was my single most important act of liberation. I met a whole new group of people, many of whom have since become close friends. I met the man who became my lover and with whom I have been living for the last year. I was able to talk about a piece of my life that had been locked away. I regretted wasting so much time. I was able to move away from simply being a boring banker and to express a more innovative part of my nature and in public.

HENRY

In the sixth form I remember being very sexually aroused by a few of the more attractive boys but I refrained from talking about this to them as I felt sure that they would be hostile if I did. In the scouts, however, I could have been more open. I joined the scouts at the very late age of sixteen for a mixture of reasons to do with improving myself, making more friends, becoming emotionally more mature and learning how to get on with other boys better. By a lucky chance, the scout group was an extremely warm and supportive one. The scoutmaster was only twenty-three, almost like an elder brother to us, and above him was a very gentle and kindly old group scoutmaster. So, in this happy and supportive atmosphere I was welcomed, accepted and quickly rose to a fairly leading position in the group. Judging from the erections which I could see plainly from some of our parades, there was quite an undercurrent of sexual feeling among some of the members of the group, although I never saw much overt expression of this, except for some very friendly rough and tumble at summer scout camps. The senior boy was very well built and sexually precocious, and delighted in telling us stories of his exploits with girls, but also he felt sexually attracted to at least one boy in the group and, on one occasion, kissed me very sweetly on the ear in a quiet corner. But, sadly, that was about as far as it went. So, although I was attracted to members of my own sex at the time, I never felt easy about this.

During my last years at university I managed to read a few books on homosexuality such as D. J. West's book and the massive work on sexuality written in Victorian times by Havelock Ellis which basically seemed to say that to be a homosexual was not too bad really. But I was profoundly distressed by two factors. One was that the image I had of gay men was that of repulsive old men in old clothes hanging around toilets waiting to seduce younger men; or of rather scruffy working-class men who did it in public toilets. I can't remember where the first image came from, but the second came from fairly regular reports of man A and man B being in court for 'gross indecency in a public place' which appeared in the local papers fairly regularly.

I persisted in a very closeted existence until early 1975, becoming increasingly accepting of the fact that I would never really show any heterosexual tendencies. I had until that time comforted myself by thinking that perhaps I would find some woman to whom I was really attracted, and would start a relationship with her, and perhaps eventually marry. But efforts in this direction always ended in being at some point in the relationship suddenly overwhelmed by a feeling of revulsion against the woman, and a feeling that the whole effort was ridiculous.

I saw a poster at the polytechnic in which I was teaching, saying that there was a gay group in existence which held regular meetings. This prompted me to discover, though I forget how, the existence of *Gay News*. Buying a copy I learnt of all the gay pubs in London, rushed off to the Bolton Arms in Earls Court, ran into a delicious young Australian at the bar, and we got chatting, and within the next three hours we were in bed together having a marvellous time. By this time it was 1975, and I was forty-one.

MARK

I quickly realized, when at college, that being gay didn't mean you were a bad person. It was an OK way to be, whatever my mother might have felt. However, there were two reasons why

I still felt it wasn't OK for me: one, Mother didn't like it; two, the only gays I knew, or knew about, were camp, screaming queens who paraded around looking and sounding like women. I couldn't imagine myself ever acting like that. I rejected such behaviour with my whole being. I was a man and I liked *men*. It never occurred to me that there must have been others like me around, who felt the same. If it had, I would not have known how to go about meeting them. I continued exclusively to date women.

One vacation I was working in an amusement arcade at home. I popped into a pub during my late afternoon break. It was quiet. I sat on a stool at the bar next to one of the few other occupants. He was a good-looking man with a moustache, about twenty-five. He turned to me and asked, casually, 'Excuse me, is there a gay bar in this town?' I suppose I went white. I tried to keep my voice from shaking when I replied, 'I'm sorry but I don't believe there is, though there have been rumours about The Admiral, but I think they're just that, rumours.' Obviously I had failed to keep my voice even and calm. I turned away to hide my shock. The man, misreading the situation, said something like, 'It's OK, I won't rape you, you know.' I could not, simply could not speak at all in reply. I wanted to tell him that, far from being afraid of him it was *me* I was afraid of. This incredible desire rose in me to talk to him, to get to know him, to. . .well, I didn't really know exactly what else. He was handsome and masculine and I wanted him so badly that I could do nothing but sit on my stool, drinking my shandy, and shake. He finished his drink with a gulp, got up and left. I could have cried. Later that night I did, with anger and frustration at my own ineptitude. How many times have I replayed that scene in my mind's eye?

I was nineteen then. Six years later I was still scared of being gay, but I knew with absolute conviction that I would never, could never be straight. A friend mentioned that he had visited San Francisco and seen the gay quarter full of gay men. It seemed to me that would be a perfect place to 'try it out', so to speak. It took me two years to save the money, but off I went. Two weeks in New York, during which I hit Greenwich Village and my first gay bar where I sat and chatted to the barman, and two weeks in California, where something finally happened to change my life forever.

I'd heard the gay area of San Francisco was called 'The Castro', but, on my street map of the city, I simply couldn't find such an area. I wondered how on earth I was to find it. Exploring the city streets on my second day I passed a porno store. Surely the person there would know where the gay area was? I went in, and checked that they sold gay porn, not just straight. They did. Nervously I approached the attractive, thirtyish man at the desk and asked for directions. He was charming, and engaged me in conversation, asking me about my home, my trip and so forth, telling me his name was Jean-Pierre and that he was French-Canadian. We talked for ages and before I left, with the required directions, he gave me a big affectionate hug. For the first time in my life I became aroused by the touch of a man. I duly found the Castro. When I got off the bus at Market Street and Castro, I couldn't believe my eyes. There, in front of me, was a street crowded with hundreds and hundreds of gay men, men of every shape, size, colour and age, a high percentage attractive and with moustaches! I was overwhelmed. For two days I wandered around in an ecstatic daze, going in all the bars, the shops, the restaurants, just looking! The third day was my twenty-seventh birthday. That afternoon I was picked up by a handsome Mexican-American waiter in the restaurant where I was eating brunch. That night I finally got to have sex with a man for the first time and, though the sex wasn't that good, I was now positive that a physical and emotional relationship with a man was what I was looking for. This was right for me.

Mind, after all those years without feeling a man's touch, I wasn't about to marry the first one who came along, and I duly didn't. Love came much later, and ended in utter heartbreak. However, it didn't turn me into a jaded cynic, either. I'm sure there'll be another one along any day now. . . .

4

Out

DAVID

The first stage of coming out is when you realize that you are gay. I remember that ever since I was about seven I was attracted to men but it wasn't until I was about twelve or thirteen that I realized that what I felt was different from the majority of boys of my age. I was very unhappy, wanting very much to be like everyone else, but getting a thrill when I said the word 'homosexual' which I'd looked up in the family dictionary.

I began sexual activity at about seventeen with other males, but did so in utter terror that someone I had sex with would declare me to be homosexual. I was having sex with probably mostly married men in public lavatories and there was not likely to be any of them pointing the finger at me since all of them were in the closet anyway, but I worried endlessly about this. It must be said, however, that it didn't stop me doing what my hormones were telling me to do.

The first person I told about my attraction to men was a girl I was going out with. She and I became very close. I wanted to go out with her but felt dishonest. Once I had told her we had a long relationship founded on honesty about what I felt. She was the first person I got really close to, who I felt I could trust with this the most terrible of secrets.

It's funny looking back that my sexuality was ever a terrible secret. After I had told my girlfriend and survived with great acceptance and a huge boost to my ego – that I could be gay and a decent person – I quickly told a few other people. My close circle of friends were told, each responding well, especially my flatmates who were very supportive despite the confusion over my relationship with my girlfriend. I only really lost one friend through telling people. He had formerly been my best male friend. He kept trying to tell me that I wasn't gay, the final straw being when he arranged a blind date with a woman for me. This showed a total lack of sensitivity to both myself and the woman involved, and a lack of acceptance of what I'd told him. I suspect this reaction was because he was unsure of his own sexuality.

The whole experience of coming out to each person was both nerve-wracking and exciting and, with one exception, a joyous occasion. Obviously the more people I told, the easier coming out became and the happier I became myself.

My family presented a different problem. If a friend rejects you, you can find other friends, but if your family rejects you, you only have one family. You also have to be emotionally resilient to survive rejection by people very close to you, and it would have been very hurtful to me had I been rejected, and therefore didn't dare to risk it. I had first told my girlfriend in November 1978, but it wasn't until July 1986 that I told my parents. I first told my brother and sister-in-law, both of whom were very surprised yet very supportive, saying they would help if I wanted to tell my parents.

I remember the day vividly, it was Wimbledon finals day, 1986. That morning I had gone to a preview of a film called *The Color Purple*, about a black American girl growing up in the 1920s in the southern USA. She had a hell of a life, yet survived it all. At the end of the film I thought, 'If she can survive all that, I can survive much less' and drove to my parents' house.

When I went in the television was on and my mother, an avid fan, was watching the end of the men's singles final. I just thought, 'When this ends, they are going to know', finally fixing the time to tell them. The time came and I asked my dad to join us in the sitting-room and started. I explained how what I was to say would clear up for them why my girlfriend and I had parted, and why I seemed to be getting distanced from them, which I didn't like. I told them I loved them and, for that reason, wanted them to know me, all of me, and not just the bits I had let them see. Shaking like a leaf, though determined, I looked at my father and said, 'I'm gay.'

My father shook, then started breathing heavily, while my mother shouted, or half-screamed, that I shouldn't be so stupid, of course I wasn't gay, they would have known, and what about my girlfriend? She went on for a minute like this while my father tried to gather his thoughts to talk about it. He told my mother to calm down and I explained that I was very happy the way I was and had never been happier and that I wanted them to understand or, at least, accept that being gay was right for me.

Over the preceding two months I had been dropping deliberate hints which neither had picked up at the time, or so I thought. From this conversation it was clear that my father had been picking them up, thus explaining his more reasoned approach to the issue. But it had hit my mother like a bombshell. I think that many of the negative things I had previously perceived about homosexuality had come from my mother and I knew that she was homophobic, so there was no reasoning or discussion with her, just irrational ranting.

Despite the fevered emotional temperature I had managed to keep relatively calm and my father, despite trembling, had managed to do likewise. I was so pleased by my father's reaction. He made it clear he didn't like the idea, that he didn't understand it, but that he loved me and that wouldn't change. There had always been an emotional gulf between my father and me, and this disappeared with my disclosure. Over the next eight months, until his death, my father and I grew very close and came to know each other and respect each other. I know that he didn't understand my being gay, but my openness gave him the opportunity of opening up to me. We had time to say what we needed to say to each other. My only regret was that I hadn't done it earlier so that we would have had more time together.

My mother? Well, she is still struggling with my sexuality but is slowly getting better. At first she was very bitter, wanting someone to blame, first me for meeting 'funny' people at college, then herself for that something she must have done. She still perceives gay as being perverted and can't get past the sexual aspect to realize that all the emotions I may feel for a lover are just the same as those of a heterosexual person. I've had relationships with both sexes and I know there isn't any difference. She is still trying to fit me into her image of 'a homosexual' rather than realizing this image may be wrong and that she may have to re-examine and change the image. Perhaps I am expecting too much, but it seems that she positively doesn't want to change, and can't see that the only way things will get better for her is if her image changes.

My other two brothers went through all my father's papers and found a book I'd given him, written by the parents of gay children. Because I'd guessed they'd seen the book I told them shortly afterwards and they were fine and very supportive. The one worry I had had with my brothers was that they may have confused gay with paedophilia as so many people do and would not be happy for me to be with their kids. Again, as in so many areas, my fears were totally unfounded and I'm still the kids' favourite uncle.

The next stage of coming out was to my employers. In January 1987 we had a national conference and I took the opportunity of taking aside the personnel manager, with whom I had a good relationship, and told her that I was gay and that, although it wasn't directly related to my work, I may at some point be forced to declare my sexuality publicly and that I would prefer the company to know beforehand. Although she had never come across such a thing in her work before she had gay male friends. She was confused as to why I had wanted to declare my sexuality, but accepted it. She asked who else in the company I would like to tell and suggested the managing director and the sales manager. I gave her the OK to tell them and suggested I tell my immediate boss. I had severe doubts about this as, although he and I got on very well, he was a strict traditionalist and didn't even like unmarried straight couples living together. I told him, none the less, after one of my assessments and he took the news marvellously. He was immediately extremely supportive, telling me it made no difference to our working relationship or to my work. He also suggested I should tell my colleagues or not, as I wanted, and that if there was any hassle from anybody he would be down on them heavily.

Again, with my work, it was my desire to be honest that started the ball rolling. I had become quite close to my colleagues but constantly hiding my sexuality created a barrier between us. Once again, all my colleagues were very supportive. They already knew me and their attitude didn't change at all, quite the reverse, some of them started asking me questions about my life, thus learning about how gay people really live as opposed to their preconceived ideas. It was illuminating for me to see how they perceived being gay, mostly as an obsession with sex without emotion, as something weird and whacky and definitely not an everyday occurrence. I think their attitudes have changed and it has been very positive for me to see these changes occur, to see knowledge replace ignorance, understanding replace unease.

MALCOLM

I was jolted both into coming out to myself and to coming out to other people by a friend, who thought I was gay, coming out to me! It was not something I had previously considered, therefore, while helping him sort out his sexuality over the course of several days, I was also having to sort out my own sexuality and decide whether or not I was gay.

Initially I came out to the friend who had caused all the trouble in the first place. He was sure I was gay anyway, so I automatically came out to him. And the second person I told was someone else who was coming out at the same time. I don't think I deliberately came out to anyone else for several weeks; rather it was found out by people. However, I did enjoy coming out at a large conference that I attended about three weeks later, with a few others in front of about one hundred and forty people, which made me feel great and proud to be gay.

However, after the conference, and returning to college, I retreated again to some extent into the closet, although partly this was to enable me to get on with some of the academic work which was piling up. I did start coming out again at Easter, attending a gay and lesbian youth group and making trips on to the scene a few times.

I have not come out to my family. I am not sure why this is. Partly I think it is because I do not know what the reaction would be. At times I think it would be all right, and others I am not sure. Apart from anything else I see my family infrequently and the opportunity to come out never seems to arise, and coming out by letter would not really work. It does make it rather difficult to stay at home since I know that I am not the person my parents think I am and that leaves me feeling guilty. They may have guessed anyway, since references to girlfriends and marriage have dried up over the last year or so although I don't know whether they will ever get round to asking. I really do not want to hurt them, although I could, of course, be doing exactly that by *not* telling them. I rarely talk about personal things to my parents, and it would embarrass me to do so.

I suppose the circle of people who do know has been fairly

limited in some respects since it has been mainly only those
people who I see as friends and who I trust. Having recently
started work away from my former friends, the situation has
changed somewhat. Now I am totally in the closet. This is really
not through choice since I find it very difficult working with
people and not telling them, but the nature of the work – residential child-care – makes it difficult since if the wrong people found
out I could be out of a job. I feel absolutely no sexual interest
towards the children under my care. Indeed, while I have been
there any sexual desire seems to have dried up. The work is hard
and the hours are long and all I feel like doing at the end of the
day and on my day off is sleeping. However, despite what I
might say, the old suspicions about gays working with children
will turn up, which would make life very difficult. In time I will
have to start coming out, for my own peace of mind, although
this would be in the longer term when I have got to know the
other staff well. In the meantime I will continue to get depressed
over working in what seems a very homophobic environment
after having lived and worked openly. Hopefully the whole of
the child-care field will not be the same, since it would make the
field unattractive as a long-term prospect, although I enjoy the
work immensely.

NORMAN

Every time you meet a new person who becomes a friend the
coming-out process begins again. Every time you start a new job
the process swings into action. A gay person never finishes
coming out, it is a relentless task which increasingly becomes a
chore. But it has to be done!

In the early stages I took the plunge with most of my friends
with the philosophy that if they didn't like what I was, the better
off I was without these so-called friends. As I became more
'professional' at it, the process became more refined. I wait until
I know the person reasonably well and they, more importantly,
know me. Usually it is no longer necessary to say to them, 'I
am gay'; they already know. Most of my coming out has taken
place in a social setting and usually with a pint of beer. I always
did and still do need an element of 'Dutch courage'.

I believe in coming out for political reasons. Only when there
is a substantial openly gay presence in society in general will we

be able to comfortably cohabit with straight society. I have been lucky in some respects in that though I have come out to my parents I do not have to live with and within their circles, I'm some three hundred miles and a sea away from all that. I realize that there are some people for whom coming out is not a possibility. As a Switchboard volunteer I have come across many cases, teenagers, married gays, who I have advised not to come out because of the massive problems it would create for them on a practical level at the time. Others I know would almost certainly be sacked or given a rough ride if they came out at work. Again, I am in a lucky position of having a profession and other gay work colleagues to give me support.

The one area I have not been able to come out in is the cricket club I play for. I can imagine the furore if they found out or were told I was gay. I suppose I'm selfish in some respects as this is an area where I would have to lose something because of my sexuality, the opportunity to play a game I love. But I console myself with the fact that I'm not close to anyone in the club and therefore don't feel I'm misleading or abusing a friendship by not letting them know the real me. Perhaps that's one of the keys to coming out. Come out if living a lie interferes with a friendship by misleading the other person.

RICHARD

I haven't come out. I was never in.

From the time I first identified as a gay man during my first sustained relationship with my speech therapist at the age of fifteen, I did not hide the fact that I was gay. Of course, there were a lot of things I did hide, specifically our relationship, since it would have got him into a lot of trouble if I hadn't, partly because of my age and partly because he would have been accused of abusing his professional situation. In fact, that relationship remained a totally closeted one with lies and secret meetings and so on.

It's funny but people who had more than the slightest acquaintance with me and who were not totally insensitive, never considered me to be heterosexual. Some of them assumed that I was asexual, and through my earliest teenage years this was the case. I knew that I had no sexual interest in women whatsoever, and didn't realize that there was an alternative.

My status at school, then the focus of my life, was similar to that of Judd in Mitchell's *Another Country* in that I was a politically active, anti-establishment figure, refusing to become a prefect to show my contempt for the system, editing the school magazine and flouting the school rules on uniform; I was camp years before I was gay. But I was allowed to be such because one mildly distinctive rebel – I was a published poet and a relatively distinguished student expected to sit for Oxbridge, which I refused to do as I wanted to go to London more than anything else in the world – showed the 'tolerance' of the school.

I go into this background to show that, in the environment I then inhabited, the idea of coming out was irrelevant. I was so far out of any category that people didn't make any assumptions about my sexuality. I don't think the staff or boys could conceive of me having sex at all – my life was so much a pose that it couldn't admit of such an unrefined appetite.

Writing this, though, I'm inclined to think that people must have assumed I was gay before I became so. Of course an outsider would say that they *knew* I was gay before I did. Only it's not that simple. If Ellman is right, then Wilde's first gay sexual experience took place in his thirties, years after composing essays like *The Relationship of Dress to Art* and *Impressions of America* which are significant examples of his so-called 'gay sensibility'. That sensibility was characteristic of his *personality* not his *sexuality* and the same was true of me. I think people made a false connection because of their preconceptions of faggotry which I fitted quite well. This is an important principle because I don't like the religious associations of the phrase 'coming out' and the almost religious significance it has for gay people. Although it's heresy – I use the word deliberately – in the gay circles I move in, I don't find the language of 'coming out' at all convincing. It is tied up with ideas of finding one's true self, of discovery and of revelation that remind me strongly of evangelical religion. I prefer to say that we *construct* our sexuality, depending in part on the circles we move in. The fact that I define myself as gay, which I do passionately, means that I never let situations occur which might prove anything else. This view has some currency among sociological types like Plummer but isn't at all popular among gay people. Gay people daren't accept this because they think it plays into the hands of those who think you're not born gay and therefore can be educated out of it; not realizing that the corollary is that you're not born straight either.

Having deconstructed the notion of coming out, I'll get back to my own life. I couldn't come out in a blaze of nail-varnish, because people were quite used to the nail-varnish already. I had a gay life centred on the university up the road from my house where I went to do my homework in the library until nine o'clock and then went to the student union where the gay society met. I enjoyed the company of people somewhat more mature than my contemporaries. I can't say my family were very interested. My mother left home, soon to divorce my father whose life centred on his work in a hospital, the Trades and Labour Social Club and the snooker hall; my brother was in care and my sister was discovering boys.

The principle I follow now, and which I think I followed then, though it's inevitable that I'm reconstructing the past in the context of my present feelings and views about myself, is not to positively come out, but never to lie about myself. In other words, wait for other people to make an assumption about me that's wrong and correct them if they do. The closest I came to coming out to my parents was openly reading *Gay News* to which I took a subscription as my seventeenth birthday present to myself. This put the onus on them to make an issue out of it if they wanted to, which they never did. By the age of seventeen my parents and my school knew I was gay, but it did not intrude on the home as, after the break-up with the speech therapist, I didn't have a regular affair, or on school as I had nothing but the most fleeting of relationships at school.

Now I am so open about myself that for a while my neighbours thought that my brother and I were lovers – we share a house. If I was entertaining a boyfriend, Mrs H would warn me that he was coming home. Of course I explained that the guy I was living with was my brother, but they thought I was lying! I don't tell everyone I'm gay. But if I haven't finished the *Gay Times* crossword at home I'll do it on the Circle Line.

I've experienced hostility at work from closet gays, some of them of high grade, who reckon that I'm rocking the boat. That's one of the worst aspects of our present situation. Divide and rule. Coming out doesn't make things easier, just simpler. It stops being your problem and starts being other people's. I do it to encourage the others.

With the homophobia related to AIDS it's also important to come out. One of the best ways to dispel a stereotype is to show that it's invalid. So many people can still say, 'I don't know any homosexuals.' Of course they do, they just don't *know* that they do. Also, because of my openness, a lot of people have sought my advice on safer sex and AIDS risks. I see coming out as a political act. It's like the position of Jews, we have the choice of passing, but how will anything change if we do?

Of course there are disadvantages. People expect you to be a spokesperson for gays, for which my reply is, 'Do tell me, I mean, I've always wondered . . . what do heterosexuals actually *do* in bed?' Also you get accused sometimes of 'flaunting it' but in my experience that means you haven't done it properly. There are ways and ways.

PHILIP

I've not come out.

I've never seen any point in my coming out. To my parents? Why upset their lives and our relationship? To my small circle of friends? They may well have drawn their own conclusions, but if their sex lives are no concern of mine, and they do not share their sexual experiences or love affairs with each other, why then should mine be of interest to them, it is no business of theirs. We have got along equably for forty years.

I am out to other gay persons, having been in CHE when it operated in this city. I remember a workshop they once had on coming out. One brave fellow said he had come out at work twice, and in both places had suffered harassment and ill effects. Being out in my place of work doesn't apply as I've been self-employed for over thirty years.

OWEN

I am homosexual and have found a strong identity of interest with the gay movement, though I've found it difficult to make many gay friends, not least because I'm afraid to declare my true sexuality for fear of the likely hostile reaction. Whether or not I'm a closet case as regards my homosexual nature is a matter of opinion. I have come out to my immediate family and much of the extended family, as well as to straight friends of old whom

I now see only infrequently. Many more people I know are either pretty sure or suspect I'm gay. I've also had cause to tell a number of young women who were seeking to get me into bed at the time. In our small community where gossip is rife, this all means that I'm 'queer' as far as quite a lot of people are concerned.

So far I have received little direct aggravation as a result of becoming known. I've had snide remarks made in my hearing when at the pub, but not for some years now. I'm no wimp and can handle myself in public. Perhaps due to a strong sense of personal pride I will respond to any verbal or physical attack in kind. My individuality is important to me; I have strong opinions on most subjects and confuse people by not conforming to any of the stereotypes. This isn't an easy path to take, but there are no easy options for me.

Truly coming out for me as a boy lover is, and will be for the foreseeable future, an impossibility. Even the limited degree of public acceptance so far achieved by homophiles which makes coming out a viable option, is totally closed to the boy lover. I have no desire to become a martyr to the cause.

Celibacy is my only viable option. I have in the past slept with both men and women, but sexual arousal was for me either difficult or impossible, so that these days I rebuff advances as tactfully as I am able. Relationships would only be possible for me if society's attitude to homosexuality becomes vastly more tolerant and an age of consent of fifteen or sixteen years. I am not interested in sex alone but in a mutually beneficial and loving relationship of some years duration with a persisting intimate friendship thereafter. Such a scenario is virtually impossible in our society so there is no point in seeking it, as even a platonic friendship, if established, would soon be destroyed with appalling consequences for both parties. To me it is ironic that sordid casual sex is available for those who seek out adolescent rentboys, being not nearly so risky, being so short-lived and impersonal, and to me totally worthless.

Outside pressures upon me are sometimes quite intense while still being apparently subtle. I do not conform to what is expected of me by either gay or straight people. To come out as gay doesn't help much in my case. An increased self-awareness, from acquired knowledge and experience, has given me strength and a growing ability to understand pressure and cope wih the vagaries of life. Though I'm not optimistic for the future, my life is not all doom and despondency; there is still much that gives me pleasure. If that were not the case I would very definitely end it myself.

GRAHAM

The first member of my family I came out to was my kid brother, because I was so curious about all the signals he gave off: clothes, magazines, the copy of *Giovanni's Room* and so on. And yes, we came out to each other. In a way that still strikes me as a little odd as this sharing has not brought us appreciably closer together. When I was in a relationshp which looked like being significant, I told my parents. I felt I did not want to keep such an important thing from them. I also felt it was high time for any subterfuge to finish and telling them was some sign of having reached a maturity of some sort in our relationship. I did not feel particularly anxious, but I knew I was putting their broad-mindedness to the test. I wrote to them; we usually write once a fortnight or so. After a day or two I telephoned and asked if they were all right. My mother said they had been a bit upset, felt a bit sorry for me, but loved me still and realized I was still old me. They came over and met my partner for a boozy meal. We have not really discussed it much since; I do not want it to be an issue, but it could be a source of growth in our relationship.

I worried a little that this might put some pressure on my gay brother, but we are fortunate in having two siblings married. In the end he started living with a man so that let the cat out of the bag, and his partner is enormously popular in the family. I came out to my sister a little while back as I had forgotten whether I had done so earlier. She was brilliant and it has brought us together, though we were always close.

People said to me that 'those who care for you do not mind, and those who mind do not care for you' about coming out as a gay clergyman. I get pretty near it in public. I am well known for my involvement with HIV/AIDS and hosted some Lesbian and Gay Christian Movement services in the church. But I do not believe in forcing people into a corner over the issue. Some detect my sexuality and want to talk about homosexuality, usually because they have gay children. Some want to be supportive, seeing oppression by the church. In the main I suspect members of my congregation are slightly curious about me, and conservative in their judgement of homosexuality as sin. The climate is not one in which I would find it easy to be as open and honest with people as I would like to be and some confidences have been breached by church members I have told. This was naive and I feel I could be held to ransom for whatever reason. I now keep my cards closer to my chest. It goes against my feeling that it is about time the church recognized that gay people exist, are members of the human race and stopped farting about. Yes, there's some frustration here; and the frightened heterosexual hierarchy does little to support or cherish us. In fact they're into doing us down, even those who reckon they're enlightened.

I would dearly like to be more out in the primary school where I work, but this seems risky, though surely some guess. At the hospital where I also work it is much less of an issue and I queen about with the many others to be found there. As a consequence of this need to be fairly discreet, I value my gay friends enormously and meet at least once a week for a pint and a lot of screamy chat. It lets off steam, and I can share my thoughts.

BILL

I started college quite happily, but being thrown into a world of young students including many good-looking men, my sexuality came up again. I was too scared to tell anyone though, especially as the boy I had sex with when I was eleven was a close friend who had come to the same college as me. As the sex between us had cooled and we had not spoken of it since, I did not want to risk losing his friendship, also to risk losing the friendship of my new college friends. I was relatively happy, as I did quite well at college and had enough good friends, both male and female, not to have to worry about sex. I watched from afar all the other good-looking students and, at last, at the end of the year, was introduced to the leader of the Gaysoc by a friend. She did not know I was gay and we had merely bumped into him and naturally she introduced us. But at least I had met him. I took appropriate steps and came out to him. The Gaysoc, however, was not that good, about eleven people from a college of eight thousand.

On the last night I came out to my best straight friend at college, Sarah. I had been fancying a guy at college for about two months and on the last night at the disco I got very drunk.

When I saw him with a girlfriend I cracked up and burst into tears and told Sarah I was gay. As she too was very drunk I don't think it registered too much. I left there and then walked home. I had never felt so happy just to be able to tell someone. I felt so good I smashed three windows as I walked home.

I managed to see Sarah again the next day before we all went home for the summer vacation and she was wonderful. Although she did not know much about gay people she listened to everything and is still a very close friend to this day. During the next two years at college everyone else found out, or I told them, and by the end of college I was a strong, fairly confident gay person.

My dad found out I was gay during that first summer holiday. After coming out to Sarah I returned home to a very boring, long summer holiday. I had to work in a canning factory to make some money and I became very depressed. It was one evening when my mother was in the other room that he came into mine and said, quite calmly, that he knew about me. He had noticed my depression and with the best possible intentions had looked in my diary and found there all the evidence about my feelings. He was marvellous about it, though it was obvious he was mildly disappointed. I was the responsible brother of the two and therefore the one to raise a wonderful set of grandchildren for my parents. But he said it was my life and he would back me up in anything I did. He also said that we should not tell my mother as she was seeing a doctor due to work strain and he did not think it was right to unleash another burden on her.

A year later my mum found out in a similar way. I was staying at a female friend's house, and she had found my diary. Not knowing whose it was she looked inside for a name and obviously found something to the effect that I was gay. On my return my dad told me about it. My mother and I hardly spoke for about six days. Luckily I returned to college a few days later and so the subject didn't crop up until Christmas when, during a brief row at home, she called me a 'fucking poof' and left the room. She later returned and cried on my shoulder for a while after which she went to bed. I never got any chance to talk to her about it but I bought her the book, *Now That You Know*, to try to help her understand. Now, although she still doesn't agree with much of my politics, she is as good a friend as any. My boyfriend and I often go to their house, and they often come here to London where I have taken them to various gay bars and clubs. My mum was also brave enough to back me up when I came out rather spectacularly to the whole of my home town when a letter I wrote to my old local paper about a particularly homophobic councillor was given a banner headline on the front page. Many friends asked her about it and she stood up for me all the way.

SIMON

I cannot remember when I first heard about homosexuality but as I come from an intellectual, literary family I suspect I knew the word and not its meaning from early on. There was a big dressing-up box which we used to play charades at Christmas parties. At the age of eight, so legend has it, I made a dramatic appearance at dinner one evening in a large picture hat, one of my grandmother's evening gowns and several ropes of pearls. Apparently, from that day on my mother was convinced I would grow up gay. My aunt tells me she was always saying it: 'The others will be engine-drivers and mountaineers, but Simon will be gay.' This even survived the occasion when I was found naked in the school grounds, aged thirteen, with one of the village girls and was expelled. We weren't doing much. It seemed the thing to do as all the other boys were talking about their girlfriends. I persuaded her to go out with me and we both took off our clothes and we just sat around and talked. I hadn't the vaguest idea what I was supposed to do and neither had she. If I'd known I probably wouldn't have wanted to do it anyway. Anyway I was put in the local state school. I missed the other school if only for those nights when the older boys had come into our beds. I was pretty when I was younger and I had no shortage of protectors.

Life at the state school had no such attractions. I was only a voyeur from then on, looking at the other boys in the changing-rooms. One older boy was blonde and golden skinned and wore a brief turquoise swimming costume instead of underwear. I never saw him naked. He would wear the costume under his clothes, then under his football shorts. I was more turned on by him in his turquoise briefs than any naked boy. But I never touched him or any other boy at that time.

Before I went to university I took a year out so I could, in my mother's words, 'get to know about life'. This consisted mainly of me lounging about and watching television. Eventually she decided to take me on a business tour she had to make round Europe. At a promotional party in Salzburg I met the man I have lived with ever since. He took me to his hotel room and I stayed the night. Next morning, my mother's only response was, 'Why did it take you so long?'

The extraordinary thing was that he lived only a few miles from the university where I was going a few months later. At first he said we shouldn't see much of one another. He liked to play the field and didn't want to be tied to one person. Also, I was going to university, and was looking forward to all the new young men I was going to meet. But we kept bumping into one another and nearly every time we ended up having sex and eventually moving in with him seemed the best thing to do.

I still hadn't come out to my father. That presented a real problem as he seldom seemed to hear a word you ever said to him. Mother had probably told him a dozen times about Freddie and me, but it wouldn't have sunk in. One day, as so often happened, out of a complete silence, he looked up from the book he was reading and, à propos of nothing, began discussing a point raised by the author as though everyone else in the room was reading the same book. I noticed he was reading Proust.

I cut across what he was saying and said, 'I've got something in common with him.' Astonished to have his train of thought interrupted he asked what that was. I said, 'What do Proust and Auden, Oscar Wilde, Somerset Maugham, Alexander the Great and Tchaikovsky, Michelangelo, Cole Porter, Noël Coward, Housman, John Gielgud and Marc Almond have in common?' He stared at me. 'Add me to the list,' I said. He still stared at me and then he said, 'Who's Marc Almond?'

Nothing more has been said on the subject though I think it did sink in. I'm much more fortunate than many others who often meet open hostility and recrimination from their parents when they come out. My mother is something else. All my gay friends want to meet her and they all adore her when they do.

5

Convenience

PETER

Ever since, by chance, I saw the possibilities of cottaging, at about the age of ten in 1933, I have been an inveterate and active participant. Then the possibilities were entirely visual: a good cock is 'a joy forever'. I was masturbated in a cottage about a year later. I did not enjoy it as the man was very unattractive, and I left as soon as it was over. I was not outraged, abused or ashamed. I told no one. As I grew up in my home town I used them as places where I could be picked up and met a few nice, helpful older men who advised me about my teenage doubts and guilt. At boarding-school, later, nothing homosexual happened to me. I used to frequent a cottage on trips to the city, again for visual pleasures. As I have recorded earlier, when I was fifteen, a policeman in my home town followed me home and told my mother all about my activities. He was, I suppose, decent about it, as I was not arrested and heard nothing more, except from Mother. For a few months I desisted, out of shame and out of consideration for her.

In those days there were no gay bars or clubs and so there was no other way, in a small New Zealand town, of meeting anyone. Anyway, it was *fun*. When I was at university in Auckland, a busy city-centre cottage was opposite a gay hairdresser's. 'The best view in Auckland,' he said as he picked me up. On separate visits I saw two of my lecturers leave this cottage. I was friendly with each of them but the sightings were never referred to. Luckily, neither of them appealed to me, though they were delightful men otherwise.

In 1948, after seeing a film, I went to the centre of my home

town but did not go to the cottage there which had been my
intention, because I saw an attractive man smoking in the street;
and we have been together ever since.

When we arrived in this town in 1949, I was delighted at the
number, the variety and the proximity of the cottages and at the
people gathered in them; London too, some months later, more
so in fact. We did a lot of touring then and it seemed that every
town of any size had one or more town cottages. Before it
became a resort I met someone in Pittenweem, Fife, and on the
Isle of Portland. 'Berlin meant boys' to Auden and Isherwood;
to me cottages meant sex.

I stopped for a while, after I was lured into one in 1961 by
two plain-clothes policemen and fined £5 the next day. But I
gradually started again, in another district we had moved to, and
for a while my partner and I explored together, usually ending
up in a threesome. It was very pleasant and nothing to be ashamed
of. Only once did we encounter trouble and that was a drunken
man who butted me on the nose and then stumbled off.

I was caught again in 1965, after, I believe, a tip-off, this time
being followed by two plain-clothes policemen. Since then I have
been much more afraid, almost monastic, not only because of the
police, but also because of gay-bashers. In each of these cases I
pleaded guilty. In the second, I resigned from school when it
appeared in the local press, but I got such good testimonials from
the headmaster and other influential friends, as well as from the
probation officer, that the magistrate gave me an absolute dis-
charge as the least he could, my having pleaded guilty. I paid
£10 costs, which is not the same as a fine. We were advised by
Anthony Grey and the Homosexual Law Reform Society who
supplied me with a good barrister.

Since my becoming older and more wary there seems to be
far less activity. Rarely do I go into a cottage for a legitimate
purpose and find another person, or even two in midstream,
though I surprised two furtive men in Cork. The last time I
encountered another man who masturbated me was in Dunoon
in Scotland in the summer of 1990. I was and still am incredulous
at its being possible there and in such prudish days.

Back to London in the old days. There was the famous 'iron
lung' in Dansey Place, W1, which they say was shut down during
a clean-up, and sold to an American who erected it in his garden!

My partner, many years ago, when on the way back to the

Cold Centre in Salisbury found a policeman standing outside a pub at 11.30 at night. He asked him if there was a Gents outside in the pub yard. The policeman took him round, shone his torch in the right places and then sucked him off, getting the point of his helmet tangled in my partner's chunky pullover. Nothing like that happened to me when I went to the Cold Centre. . . .

GRANT

I have never found sex in toilets to be that much of a turn on. Some of my friends, however, find that it is the only way for them to really enjoy sex. It isn't that I object to sex in them as such. I have never liked using public toilets, even when I was a child at school; if I could I would always hold on until I got home. My reason, I don't like the smell of them. Stale urine does nothing for me. The sights, yes, the smell, no.

Another reason is the story my mother told me when I was about five or six. She told me that a boy about my age had gone into the toilet at the traffic island that we were on and some men in there had cut off his penis and he had died from the loss of blood. I believed my mother totally; today I'm not sure if she was telling me the truth or trying to warn me in a round about way about gay men. In my imagination, I saw this gang of men, waiting down there to cut off my penis. On the few occasions that I used it, I never saw anyone else in there. Even today, I can't cross that island without thinking of that story, even though the toilet has been gone for at least fifteen years.

What I did do and still enjoy is reading the walls and looking at the pictures, although today they are cleaned a lot more frequently and thoroughly. I learned a lot from them, especially when I was in my early teens and knew what was what and what I really wanted.

I used to hang around the cottage in the park near to my godparents' house. I would always visit them a lot during the summer holidays. I would sit on the bench outside hoping that someone would come and chat to me. No one did apart from a young park-keeper. He asked me questions about cottages. I took that to be a warning and stayed away for a while. Then a couple of weeks later I read in the local paper that he had been done for indecent assault. I missed my big chance, because he was great looking and well hung.

I think that a lot of guys cottage because they are addicted to it. The sex that they do elsewhere doesn't give them the same high, perhaps because that's the first place they had sex. For married gays, it's probably the only place they can go without too much suspicion attaching to them. In some smaller towns it's the only place to meet people. I think that the danger adds a certain thrill to it. Why do 'breeders' do it in car parks if not for the thrill of it? The reasons why they have sex in the open are the same for us.

I do like sex in the open. When I lived in Hammersmith there was a part of the river bank that was great. A lot of the student nurses from Charing Cross Hospital went there, among others. Ah, happy days. Also, the bushes in Brighton were a good place to meet. A lot of the time the guys wouldn't bother going into the bushes, but would have sex on the path; the more daring under the lighting. I learned a lot from watching them.

SCOTT

Cottaging repulses me for two reasons. One is that I don't care for casual sex. The other is that it is so aesthetically unappealing. People have invited or exhorted me to go cottaging, tempting me with the peculiar glamour of the sordid, the spice of danger and the protection from 'getting involved' with other people.

When I was in my early twenties, I was pestered by a weirdo who alternately and/or simultaneously tried to 'straighten' me out, sell me the so-called celibate life, encourage me to suicide *and* sexually molest me himself. He also tried very hard, at one stage of his persecution, to convince me that cottaging was the only way gay men ever met. I suppose he did this either to make me do something I found distasteful or to keep me lonely.

I have always tended to avoid public lavatories since then. I deplore all the *agent provocateur* and policemen-in-broom-cupboard techniques. Nevertheless I believe that sexual solicitations can be a great nuisance to people – especially, perhaps, to gay people – who only enter to empty their bowels or bladders. I do believe that a small fine, without the attendant publicity and scandal, should be retained as a token legal penalty. Perhaps, if the spice of danger were reduced to such a token, there would be less cottaging.

I must admit to having had sex in a public place, though it

was far less public than most public conveniences. I had been corresponding with a boy – he was twenty-four and I was twenty-eight – who lived in a certain Surrey commuter town. One Sunday afternoon I went out to meet him. He led the way to a quiet churchyard where we sat on a bench and talked. After an hour or so he began coming on strong. He persuaded me to follow him through the fence into a narrow strip of woodland beyond which rose a railway embankment. There was a little embracing, but after a couple of kisses he told me to stop. He allowed me to put my hand inside his shirt for just as long as it took to get an erection. From his side, his attention was almost exclusively on my penis, not my most attractive feature to my mind. I think the only reason I went along with this was that I was taken by surprise. I wanted to get it finished with so we could get back to our conversation. Also, I was very lonely and unhappy at the time, and would have put up with a great deal to nurture anything that looked like a worthwhile relationship. Anyway, I was too nervous to come to orgasm but I brought him to it. As soon as that was over, he was in a great hurry to adjust his clothes and clear out. Not only did he leave the church-yard, but made excuses about having to get back home. He seemed full of remorse and self-reproach. We corresponded for a while after this. When I suggested another meeting, he replied, 'Not just yet. We went too far.' I wrote the last letter in our correspondence, which ended without a second meeting. I some-times believe that, if only I'd refused, we might still be friends, if not lovers.

JON

Occasionally, between the ages of thirteen and sixteen, I would attempt to cottage. I don't think I knew of Joe Orton, but maybe I knew from sensationalist tabloid trash that there was something I wanted and might enjoy in that enclosed male-only environ-ment.

One afternoon in the local park I followed a man around to the wooded area after eye contact outside the loos. We ventured into the cemetery and he beckoned me between two graves into the trees. I bottled out, telling myself he could be crazy and want to hack me to pieces. This happened on one or two other occasions until I made eye contact with a chap in the toilets in the centre of town. He waited outside and kept waiting. I walked past him. I was simultaneously excited and terrified. However, this occasion put me off being a possible cottager. It was nothing dramatic but he got in his car and followed me, kerb-crawling at first, then accelerating as I tried short cuts and ultimately running from him. I'd convinced myself he was a plain-clothes copper and boy was I in the shit. I ran to a neighbour's house so he wouldn't know where I lived. It freaked me out so much it stopped being sexy. My cottaging experiences stopped there really.

Our local park was big and woody and sometimes I used to ride my bicycle nude around midnight hoping something would happen. It never did. Rolling nude in the snow was also a favourite, on the way home from a club in the winter on my own. Nothing ever happened. My best memory of outdoor sex was a bit of mutual (safe) buggery, just in boots, in the middle of the day in the later summer, with the sun glinting through the leaves of the forest. We ran naked through the trees, rubbing against the bark, and rolled in the leaves, sleeping out in a tent. However, this was with a lover so maybe it doesn't count.

Sometimes I think it's a bit sad that some men can only get to meet others in cottages and that it's a bit degrading. But then again, it does hold the excitement, the thrill of being public, rebellious, illegal and with strangers. I get angry when I think about people being driven to it by the continued social unacceptability of being gay and the ghettoization of social places for gay men.

They're shutting the loos in Brighton at the moment. I wonder why, the bastards. Before the one close to where I work was shut I popped in on the way home for a piss. I wandered in on two chaps, one on his knees in the lock-up with the door left open, sucking the other who was facing him. I was a little surprised but said, 'Don't mind me', but they both ran. I felt a bit bad as a member of our invisible family. I just hoped they went off somewhere together afterwards.

I do believe in public kissing, on the basis that people must be constantly reminded that we're everywhere, and I'm not going to censor my behaviour to avoid offence. This, of course, does have its limits. I might wait until the four lads have gone past before kissing a mate goodnight, but that's common sense and plain survival. On starting my job at the library I invited my gay male friends to pop in and kiss me over the counter to aid my coming out. This did actually make one woman face her prejudice and raised several student eyebrows.

There has been quite a bit of queerbashing in Brighton recently. A close friend said he'd been beaten for the second time last week. He tells the police but they have a bad reputation here. About a year ago on a murder enquiry they took lots of information from the gay community in 'strict confidence'. This has since been used in another case which resulted in a queerbasher getting off. Would *you* trust them?

GARETH

Aged twelve I was taken to London for the day by a family friend. At one point I went to the cottage in Oxford Circus underground and became aware of at least one man, probably in his thirties, displaying a hard-on near me. I had never seen an erect cock before and did not realize how large they could be so I thought the man must be ill, physically because of the unusual size and mentally for flaunting his disability in public.

The next significant occasion was when I did realize what cottaging was all about. I was in my late teens and on a shopping trip to a new town with my mum. I went into the cottage in the town centre and there was a large man next to me with a hard-on. I felt horny and let him wank me off. When I went outside my mum showed some concern at the time I'd taken. 'All right?' she said.

There was just one occasion that I sensed the excitement some people feel. There are two famous cottages on the A45 between Birmingham and Coventry almost opposite each other on the dual carriageway. They were so famous they had a nickname, which I forget. At that point the road passes through countryside. Once I stopped there at dusk and saw hares jumping through the fields alongside. The night I'm thinking of I'd been to a club in Leicester or Coventry and decided to call in on the way home. Inside it was black; all the bulbs had been put out of action. Gradually two or three guys emerged. I recognized one of them as someone I had fancied for some time and who was really hot. He became the centre of a knot of guys, fucking and sucking.

They were all clones.* I found the clone look a turn-on anyway and I really enjoyed generally messing around with them. But it was the start of the AIDS scare, so I did not fuck with them.

But I rarely go cottaging. It's usually smelly, furtive and boring and not worth the risks of police entrapment. I have been lucky and never had any trouble of this kind. It seems to me that the risk of arrest is in proportion to the amount of cottaging you do. Besides I now work in a place with a large park and enjoy cruising around there in sunny weather. It's always busy in the afternoon rush hour and on weekend afternoons so there is plenty of choice. I prefer the fresh air and the chance to get a good view before I make a move. There are also probably a lot more younger guys there than would be prepared to go cottaging. This appeals to me.

CHRISTOPHER

Cottaging has been part of my life since I became sexually active. As to my attitudes towards it, they are a little ambivalent. On the one hand I cannot condemn it without being a hypocrite, as it was, and still is, an important part of my life; on the other hand, I wish there had been a more socially acceptable and less compulsive way to start my gay life. When I started cottaging it was the only way I knew to make contact with other gay men. I knew nothing of the pub or club circuit or other organizations and I didn't until I had the courage to buy my first copy of *Gay News*. I wish I had been told more about this at school and possibly had an older, more experienced man to show me the ropes. I used the word 'compulsive' above because it was very much like a drug for me; I would spend whole lunch hours waiting in an empty cottage for someone to turn up, or spend an afternoon supposed to be spent in a museum or art gallery in and out of the cottage. I got very depressed when I didn't make it with anybody, and the same if I *did* make it with someone who I didn't really like but who was just there. I got very tense if the cottage I was going to was shut, and suffered something akin to withdrawal symptoms. I find that if I've been on a cottag-

* In the mid-1970s, as a reaction to a perceived effeminacy, it became the fashion for gay men to have short hair and moustaches and wear American lumberjack type shirts and jeans. The term 'clone' was initially derisive but eventually became an acceptable self-definition.

ing binge my concentration suffers, as if I've been draining my energy.

In moderation, however, it can give one a real buzz, set the heart racing and give a real boost to one's energy, as if one's bodily systems have been given a boost, which of course they have, and then a nice relaxed feeling after. The difference between the two is that when it's compulsive, one is doing it because one feels one has to, even if the situation and one's bodily state is not appropriate, and one is overly emotionally involved with the success or failure of the attempt, whereas in the case of the occasional visit the opposite is true and the result is something which is integrated with the rest of the day's activities.

As to the attractions of cottaging, these are various. Firstly, you don't know what kind of person you are going to meet and this can create a sense of anticipation, a feeling that any of one's fantasies can be fulfilled. Personally I find the workmen from the building sites near where I work the most exciting, these butch guys so outwardly straight in their boots and overalls who love to come in and have their cocks and buns felt and more. Often apparently married – they wear gold bands – there is the feeling of a need to drain excess energy which is quite exhilarating. Then there is the smart city type in his grey or blue suit. If I'm really lucky I find someone with a place to go back to. I prefer this in many ways because, although cottages are exciting, in many ways they can be dangerous and uncomfortable.

RICHARD

Cottaging as a means of self-discovery did not really exist for me when I was at school. It wasn't important to me or my gay mates and we didn't discuss it, except in a joking way. I was a fairly mature out young man when I went cottaging for the first time, although naive about the possible consequences as far as being in conflict with the law was concerned. Although I've never had any personal experience of police tactics *vis-à-vis* cottaging, I know people who have and it's devastated their lives. This is quite wrong. Cottaging is largely invisible to anyone not involved in it and it's quite incorrect to characterize it as a 'public nuisance'.

Up to then I had come to associate cottaging with furtive, closeted homosexuality, with older or more conservative men, perhaps married, who sought to enjoy gay sex without facing the consequences of their sexuality. I considered such people as self-oppressed and cowardly, and it was a side of gay life that I distinguished sharply from my own. This attitude only changed when I came to consider cottaging as an *activity* rather than as a sexual lifestyle; it was something that anyone, myself included, might do.

My main reason for not cottaging is that they are such sordid places. Public lavatories are dismal at best, and the ones that become cottages are often the worst of the lot. I wonder why? I've never known anything to happen at Stockwell, one of the most well-appointed conveniences, whereas cruddy Baker Street is, in Alan Bennett's words, if not exactly a rosette, at least two crossed knives and forks.

When I have cottaged it has been for two specific reasons. The first is when I'm in places with no other way of making sexual contacts. For that reason I went cottaging in – or rather under – Red Square, Moscow; Kreshatik Avenue, Kiev; and alongside the Peerie Sea, Kirkwall. In Kirkwall and Kiev this provided me with an *entré* into a gay world I'd never have discovered otherwise.

The other situation is where I come home feeling really depressed, with no messages on the answering machine, and that feeling can be lifted by being found sexually desirable by a stranger, something which does wonders for my self-esteem. Perhaps it's not therefore surprising when I say I've never developed an enduring relationship out of such a contact.

An incident. Several years ago my friends Karl, Toby and I were on the tube when Toby confessed he had never been cottaging. 'All right,' Karl said, winking at me, 'let's do it now.' 'Sure,' I enthused, 'let's make it a cottage crawl.' Toby looked horrified. With our travelcards we 'did' the Circle Line clockwise from Baker Street. Nothing very much happened, largely because Karl and I were very boisterous and we were only doing it to wind up Toby, whom we both considered to be sexually inexperienced despite his protestations to the contrary.

I have had sex in other public places, from the banks of the Danube and Westerplatte in Gdansk, to the beach at Ayr, as well as the better known haunts like Clapham Common and Hampstead Heath. Hungary was particularly memorable, as nothing could have been further from my mind than sex when I left the restaurant in Budapest and walked to the river to admire the old city of Buda before returning to the station for my night train. Suddenly I realized that the square I was in, slightly lower than the surrounding ground and well planted with shrubbery, was full of fornicating men and that a guy in a leather jacket and dark glasses, quite incongruous for a dark October night, was cruising me. The experience of fucking in the middle of Budapest, the rattle of trams and the wail of boat horns in my ears, is one I shall never forget. What made me feel good afterwards was the affirmation of sex between two men who differed in everything – race, language, background – except being gay.

DAVID

The first time I got my hands on a real man I was two weeks past my seventeenth birthday and rather physically immature. I drove my parents' car to the main post office to post letters as a demonstration of my newly obtained driving licence. I posted the letters and went into the public lavatories next door. I shut the door and sat down to do what I'd come for. Suddenly I realized that the wall of the cubicle to my right had a large circular hole right through to the next cubicle. I leant back and peered through to see pink skin with dark hair on legs, seated next door. Moving forward I saw that this was a real man and he was wanking. I was overwhelmed with a desire to touch his cock. I'd never had a focus of desire before. I could hardly breathe with excitement, or was it fear? I don't know. Anyway the man got up and pushed himself through the hole – I couldn't believe it was happening – I touched its firmness and warmth and was literally dizzy with the reality of it all. I couldn't have done that much for him and he withdrew and signalled that I should reciprocate. Without a moment's thought, I did and suddenly found a warm wetness. It was great and yet I was frightened and so I pulled back. A piece of paper and a pen appeared through the hole. 'Can we meet?' I was horrified and returned them. 'What age are you?' came back the note. Thinking of my physical immaturity I wrote, 'Just sixteen', and sent back the message. 'Put your dick through,' came the reply. I did so and within a few seconds I came with collapsing knees. I was overwhelmed with fear and loathing. I knew that it was exactly what I wanted, but also that it branded me as a homosexual. I have never dressed and run from a place as fast.

I was certain I had the mark of the homosexual on me. I ran

and ran to get away from him and the place, terrified he would see my face (neither of us had seen the other's face) and tell the world I was a homosexual. I sneaked back to the car and drove with wildly shaking legs, a danger to other road-users, for several miles to a nearby village – to make an alibi? Swiftly parking the car I jumped out and walked straight into a friend from school. I stammered and stuttered, my eyes roving the street, I suppose, looking for the man who must be following, and tried to continue a conversation. My friend looked puzzled; the look on her face asked, 'Why is he behaving so strangely?' but she was too polite to articulate it. 'Why can't she see in my eyes what I've done? Why can't she see the homosexual sign over my head which had appeared the moment I slammed the door on that toilet cubicle. Why can't she see how I've changed?'

The experience was both exhilarating and frightening, not happy not sad. I knew from then on what I wanted to do and continued to do it. My family thought I had developed a helpful streak as I so frequently volunteered to take mail to the post office. This went on for another year until I went to university but, by then, I had broadened my horizons to practically any public toilet in the central belt of Scotland.

IAN

Unlike many of my gay friends I had no direct experience of cottaging until I had been on the gay scene for some years. I think the first time I had sex in a cottage was while changing trains in a railway station in Italy. An attractive young man stood next to me at the urinal and subsequently motioned me to go into a cubicle where we quickly had sex. That has been my only experience of sex in a cubicle. Although I know the sordid surroundings and element of danger are a turn-on for many men, they were not for me.

However, I have picked up men in cottages and gone elsewhere with them for sex on a number of occasions in various locations. For a while I felt guilty about this and I found it hard to reconcile with ideas of gay pride and putting across a dignified and positive image of gay life. Probably what changed my opinions was knowing several men who were very open about cottaging, yet balanced and sorted out people.

Of the men I have met in this way – at a guess I would say

we are talking of about perhaps twenty or thirty over a seven-year period – quite a high proportion have been, I suppose, social misfits in the sense that contacts other than through cottaging would not have been easy for them. Quite a few have been married or living with their families, thus with nowhere to take people back to, and frightened of going to gay clubs. I have been struck as to how closeted these people were, clearly guilt-ridden about their homosexual feelings, while others have been remarkably open about their double lives.

Several of the men I have met in this way have become friends. Two of these, both intelligent and handsome men who are aware of the gay scene and would have no trouble making contact with other guys in a bar are more or less addicted to cottaging and have regaled me with many stories of close encounters with the police. Both I suspect have become so used to cottaging that they would find it difficult to relate sexually to men they had not first met in a cottage; perhaps too there is an element of not being able to bother with chatting up men in clubs when all that can be avoided in a cottage. Cottaging does not repel me as it once did. I accept it as one form of sexual expression, but hardly an ideal one. Self-respect as a gay man and a feeling of solidarity with the gay community at large are very important to me and I now prefer, and am lucky enough to be in a position to be able to prefer, to make sexual contacts through recognized gay venues. There is no moral judgement here, it is a straightforward personal preference.

My first experiences of gay bars and clubs were in London in 1974. The first club I went to was the Festival Club where I was taken by an older friend. It was extremely disappointing. What made a particular impression was its location and the approach to it. We turned off St Martin's Lane into a dark and very narrow alleyway. The club was some way down, hidden away, and the atmosphere seemed sleazy. Yet inside there was a distinct feeling of respectability. It was much as I imagined a 'gentleman's club' to be. There was an open fire with a number of middle-aged – or so they seemed to a sixteen-year-old – men sitting round. My friend spoke to some of them about opera. I felt completely alienated and never went there again. Another friend took me shortly afterwards to the A & B, which stood for 'Arts and Battledress' I believe! This was somewhere in Soho, I forget where, but again seemed to be tucked away in a back street so that one entered feeling furtive and rather excited, not quite knowing what to expect. This was a much livelier place and, although quite small, was full of men dancing and having a good time. I enjoyed the visit although, again, I never went back.

Soon afterwards I moved to a provincial city where the only gay club became a regular haunt. As there was no competition I had a love–hate relationship with the place which was tatty and run–down, but could be fun sometimes. It seemed a rabbit warren of passages and staircases and was surely a terrible fire-trap. There were silly regulations about having to pretend to eat a meal after pub closing time. This was rigidly enforced by the staff who were rather camp and prickly though not entirely unfriendly, so plates of liver and mashed potato and the like had to be taken by every customer only about 10 per cent of whom would ever eat them. I made a number of friends there. I relished the fact that it was altogether another world to the one outside. There I felt able to be relaxed about being gay in company. But I was also aware of how unfriendly it could seem to newcomers without any friends or contacts.

Of gay bars rather than clubs, the ones that stick in my mind most from my first year of coming out are the Salisbury in St Martin's Lane, another venue where the gay and the artistic overlapped, which I went to a number of times, and the Union Tavern in Camberwell where I saw my first drag act. I was taken there by another friend who loved drag shows, but I hated it; not the idea of drag, but the crudity of the jokes and the way the audience seemed to find the costumes so wonderful. Then there was my one and only trip to a gay pub in Croydon on a memorable winter's night with a very boring man I had met through a gay youth group, though he was at least twice my age. His ancient car had to be started by cranking it up by hand, and it broke down several times on the way to and from the pub as it was freezing cold. As I had to keep pushing the car I caught a terrible cold which was with me for weeks. The pub was just very dull and quiet and as my companion had no conversation at all and sat puffing at his pipe all evening, I felt bored and depressed. However, while my companion was in the gents a young ginger-haired man in a fur-trimmed coat came across and spoke to me briefly, handing me his telephone number. He subsequently became my first lover.

Sixteen years later I'm back in London and gay bars do play

some part in my life. If I were asked to choose the best bar, my favourite would be the Market Tavern. I first went there about six years ago on Gay Pride day and thought it was wonderful: lots of attractive men, good music, unpretentious decor, two bars for variety, space to dance. For worst bar I think I would choose the Brief Encounter in St Martin's Lane, always crowded, smoky and a very transient clientele.

My motives for going to a pub or club are mixed – meeting old friends and possibly meeting new ones are uppermost, but dancing, drinking and cruising are other factors. The gay environment itself is a stimulus and, after a week or two without it, it comes as a pleasant change to feel the solidarity of an all-gay crowd.

KEVIN

The main difference between gay and straight sexual activity is that gay men have no rules and traditions. The reason why many heterosexuals are alarmed and even repelled by homosexual activity is because they expect gay men to follow *their* rules and traditions, and gay men are having none of that. Prolonged polite meetings, courtship and monogamy are unnatural practices after all; passion and satisfaction the most natural in the world. In a sexual meeting of two men proximity and need may be the only relevant factors; looks are a bonus. Intelligence, conversational ability, bank balance, commitment, diligence, steadfastness, social graces and responsibility are way down the list. They become relevant only if a relationship develops beyond the purely physical.

The phenomenon of cottaging may well have developed here had there been no legal constraints. Passionate sexual activity needs only the commitment of the moment. It doesn't require a chat-up process or the exchange of credentials. What it needs is a venue. The public lavatory is perhaps the ideal place. The sight of another man's penis, either erect or flaccid, is often enough to arouse a gay man. The act of exposing his penis in a place where others are present and likely to see it, is often enough to arouse any man. Taking this extremely low threshold of sexual impulse, is it surprising that so many have acted on it? Thus the very nature of a public or communal urinal is implicitly a sexual place.

Because sexual activity between men was a criminal offence for so long, it was only the brave or foolhardy who would run or attend gay bars and clubs and only in major cities where there was anonymity in everyday life. Public lavatories, together with a few open-air cruising areas, were the *only* places most gay men could meet. That others could be repulsed by this is perhaps understandable. Such places are seldom the most savoury of environments. But it is the local authority that should be criticized here for not enforcing proper standards of hygiene, not the users. The other seemingly unsavoury element is that these places are reserved for those most private and unspoken functions of human life, and though these functions are natural in themselves to some it seems unnatural and unwholesome to associate sexual impulse with defecation; but, then, to many anything between the legs is lavatorial and, therefore, repulsive.

Given the choice of meetings in public lavatories and in a pub or club I have no doubt of my own preference. Until my early twenties I had no choice; it was the lavatories or nothing. Later, given the alternative of a warm, interestingly lit place with music and conversation, I gradually grew to want to avoid those dark, dank smelly places where it was often cold enough to freeze your balls off. It is interesting, though, how this single tradition persists, this need for the village pump. Many when cruising in a bar today still feel the need to make the actual contact at a urinal. Eye contact is made in the bar, a smile, a wink, a knowing look, whatever. Then one will make an excuse to go to the loo the other following at a discreet distance; credentials are exchanged with penis exposure and dates made or denied. I can never be bothered with all this, in fact I make a point of never using the lavatories in bars unless urgently pressed. My contention is that, if a potential partner can't say hello to me in a gay bar, without all that pretence, then there's no hope for us in bed. However, I am no hypocrite. I readily admit it was in the lavatories in London's Leicester Square that I met the one true great love of my life.

I want to say some more about pubs and clubs. The pub I know best is the Coleherne in Earl's Court which is the only surviving pub traditionally to cater to the leather crowd. The wearing of black leather: jackets, chaps, caps, boots is wrongly identified with S/M sex. If its roots were, in the past, exclusively with *aficionados* of S/M practices, then the image has been hijacked. The leather crowd is a reaction aginst perceived effeminacy. Leather signals lack of inhibition, a promise of sex without bourgeois rules or restrictions, the guarantee of raunch. A further system of signalling with flags – coloured handkerchiefs worn in one back pocket or another – left no doubt as to the wearer's preferences. Left-hand dark blue: I fuck you; right-hand dark blue: you fuck me, and so on.

In the middle 1970s on a Saturday night you needed a shoe-horn to fit another person in the Coleherne bar. Because everyone was jammed together the most outrageous acts of intimacy took place. Habitués developed the impassive look designed to camouflage anything happening from the waist down. The final bell then wasn't the signal for a rush to the bar to cajole a final pint, but the cue for the pulling up of trousers, the zipping, the buckling of belts.

In those days there was always overt sexual activity in the lavatories of pubs and clubs. The natural development was the provision of specifically designated areas for sex. Back rooms, as they were called, were already established in more sexually liberated countries such as America and Holland, but in Britain, where sex between men when there are more than two people present, not in a locked room, is still criminal activity, it seemed unlikely that they would ever be a reality. But there was a burgeoning of defiance in the late 1970s that proclaimed we have the right to do with our bodies in consensual activity whatever we want. It was paradise for a while. The back rooms flourished.

Again, back-room sex was not a favourite activity of mine. But again I would be a hypocrite if I said I never used them, but I went to those bars primarily because they attracted the men who attracted me. I loved the atmosphere. It was daring and provocative, essentially and entirely male, our rules, our traditions in the making. One bar had a system where, if the police arrived at any door, someone pressed a switch and suddenly all the lights in the back room went on; additionally a rotating police-light would flash! That was the kind of defiant humour of the time. Of course, when it arrived, that other uninvited and unexpected guest, HIV, was, invisible to all, having a field day. No one then knew of the potential devastation and when that became clear the back rooms closed. But I am certain this is a temporary hiatus. When the crisis is averted, the need for the celebration of male sexuality will again be recognized and there will be those to cater for it.

AIDS has not cancelled out gay sexual freedoms; natural impulses will always be acted upon. If anything, cottaging appears to be on the increase; the men who moved out of the back rooms had to go somewhere. And the cruising areas are still cruised. (Oh, that deep midwinter's day when the two of us, stark naked, had passionate sex in the snow. . . .) Back rooms pop up and are closed by alarmists. (I remember how moved I was at one such where everyone was using condoms.)

In the assumption that gay men would follow the rules and traditions of established heterosexuality after 1967, heterosexual society was ignoring the fact that these rules and traditions existed only from convenience to give order and direction to civilization. In fact gay men rebelled against what they saw as an aping of heterosexuality. Through open debate and discussion, a gay sensibility emerged; there were rights to be fought for. And of all those rights the most fundamental is the right to allow that sensibility to evolve without fear or recrimination, following its own rules. Where this harms no one and fulfils many, how could there be any rational objection?

6

Together

JULIAN

Politically I want to be recognized in, for instance, a census as a unit of the population with my lover. Wouldn't it be nice knowing, to the nearest half-dozen that, yes, there is a healthy 10 per cent of the population living in faggotry? That doesn't mean that I view partnership as the equivalent of marriage, though it can be. There must be something fundamentally, inwardly different. Outwardly the partnerships of two men or of a man and a woman may look similar. Possibly even in the former wifely roles might be assumed in which one partner does the things associated traditionally with the woman's part in marriage, like washing, cooking or the weekly shopping trip. The living together of two individuals, and the gradual loss of individuality. But it doesn't have to be that way. I *want* to be seen in coupledom, to supermarket on Sundays and to proclaim a loud defiance of the heterosexual marriage. Straights don't, after all, shop with the *panache* of male lovers. Out shopping you'll see us enjoying ourselves, expressing our faggotry through the supermarket trolley.

Twelve days ago Neil and I met up again. The words 'met up' suggest intention, perhaps misleadingly. The truth of the matter is that we'd met only once or twice before, a couple of years ago when Robert and I had been staying with George, his lover and an ex of Robert's. That Saturday morning found me cruising a guy at a pub-bar in Edinburgh, at around 3 am, and trying hard to pluck up the courage to go over and say hello. I didn't, as it turned out, have to, since it turned out that we knew each other already. I confess an initial feeling of disappointment at the thought that all the cruising had been pointless, since we knew each other, and wouldn't therefore be getting into bed together; a pity, I thought, and was wrong.

The relationship with Neil *is* a long-term one, a long-term relationship that's only been going for a few days. It has developed quickly, I his intra-muscular, subcutaneous, long-term potential live-in lover, he mine, a walking, talking, fucking miracle. He phones from work once or twice a day, we make plans for the future, losing the sense of insecurity – will he *really* be back tomorrow? – of the first week, deciding to live together and do great things, to become an Edinburgh David and Jonathan, a bear and his boy. Yesterday he brings with him a poem, a love poem, the first I've ever had. . . .

What, though, distinguishes the relationship, the long-term relationship, from a quick pick-up? What would allow me to claim that our first night together, actually a weekend, was the first night of something that will go on a very long time? *Why* do I love Neil and why, approaching irrationality, does he love me? Is there a difference between love, and being in love? Questions that become realities. Did sex precede the opening of our relationship, open it or what? Was Neil a prospective lover when we met, or a friend, or both? He was someone I knew quite vaguely, just well enough to remember that I liked him, and that Robert and I had wanted to remain in touch with him whatever the outcome of his relationship with George. A boy with bright eyes, a frank smile and sense of humour and interest. I hadn't imagined going to bed with Robert's ex's ex, still less on a permanent basis. Thinking about it, I'm glad that I did cruise him before finding out who he was. I'm going out with a stranger with whom I have something in common, rather than an ex of an ex of an ex.

Love, as they say, changes everything, behaviour as well. One might, I suppose, risk losing one's identity, of forgetting that one is loved for who and what one is rather than being an impossible stereotype of idealized behaviour. I do find it tempting to behave well, in a way calculated to please my lover for whom, to use a cliché, there is nothing that I would not do. I hope that rather than *losing* identity, I *acquire* something of his and also of the identity of a lover. One is vulnerable in love, which means opening out to new experiences and, best of all, the opportunity of experiencing someone else, looking at one's own life through another's eyes.

Jealousy is a problem, associated mentally with the possessive style of the heterosexual liaison. Rationally I know that it would make sense for my lover to look elsewhere to satisfy sexual and social tastes that I can't satisfy, to fuck the buns off a bank clerk for the night, whatever, so why then should I derive pleasure from my highly charged, highly sexed lover pledging even sexual fidelity, or a twinge of pain at the thought of his bedding someone else tonight? No doubt I'll over-compensate for the jealousy, to the extent even of encouraging him to explore. Our second night together was, as it happened, a threesome with a flatmate. . . .

When Robert and I split up we worked hard at the divorce, trying to salvage a friendship from what hadn't worked as love. Divorce became the most successful, and least conventional part of our relationship, something we did that we had no models for. Now we are better friends than we were lovers, at least I think that's true, if not it's a consoling fiction. As I explained to Robert's new lover I no longer think of him as being my ex. A major shift of perception. I kept a sporadic diary that re-read now seems maudlin as well as painful. Here is what happened on Saturday, 1 July 1989.

Thirteen months since I met Robert. Probably won't do a card this time round; every day thirteen months ago was unexpected; then about six months ago we'd started celebrating on a monthly basis; and after marking a year (last month) that scale seems okay as long as there are other reasons for getting out the champagne. There's still a bottle in the fridge. It would be nice to have some really good news as an excuse to open it. It's in the fridge ready for the eventuality.

Let's begin with yesterday, Friday, it led into today after all. Mornings and evenings are now dominated by trying to get Robert into bed for a fuck, the working day by wondering why not and whether it might happen when he gets in. Nothing's happened since last Thursday. We've hardly touched each other except accidentally in bed. I feel uneasy at initiating sex and would like to caress him without feeling that I should be keeping my hands to myself. Wonder why when he goes out to work he's stopped kissing me, why when he gets in he doesn't kiss me. Quite easy to have very little contact with him in twenty-four hours especially if he's up early and I'm back late. The question of whether the relationship will last is carefully kept at the back of my mind, which is where I want it.

On the way to the market I buy *Gay Times* and *Vulcan*, the latter for the first time and prompted by having discovered Robert's soft porn a few weeks ago. Thought then, probably with relief, that Robert isn't such a damned puritan, and have since been trying adolescently to demonstrate that I'm not. We discussed the matter. I'd read too many agony aunt letters that treat pornography (i.e. 'I've just discovered that my husband reads. . .') as a problem to pass off the chance of a discussion, and I was also treating it as one. I think that's now resolved.

I go out to the pub at around 8.30, half an hour before Robert who's waiting for a phonecall from Dave, a friend of his from college. It struck me that I hadn't been out alone for months. It seems odd and difficult to stand on my own at the pub for a few minutes. Robert comes in just after nine. I see again how wonderfully elegant he is. Start thinking that he's not really happy here – i.e. with *moi*, and that he should be attracted to Jim, who is sitting at the same table, if he's any sense. Odd, thinking that one's own lover and virtually a complete stranger would make a positively nice couple.

Alex, Robert's ex, joins us, making an effort all night to be cheerful. He's just quit his job and has started temping at the place where Robert works. Jim also works at the hospital, and a male nurse, who knows everyone vaguely and probably Jim intimately, is sitting with us, so quite a lot of the conversation is about micro-biology, urine, poo and serology. I start feeling irritated with or, if I'm being nice, *concerned* about Alex: he's an unhappy bunny. Also I say to myself that I hope he'll settle down with someone, which is patronizing, and then add, mentally, 'like me and Robert', and, physically, put my arm around Robert. I try harder than usual not to feel that Alex is jealous of Robert and might not like seeing us together.

At closing time something's obviously wrong with Alex, and Robert says he has to have a few words with him and that he'll catch me up on the way back. So I have to walk home alone, which is also odd, so I wait outside shops on the way back thinking Robert will catch me up, and then feel a bit embarrassed at standing queenily in the street. I reflect on infidelity, possibilities thereof, Robert, me, someone else, and what to do if one found out.

When Robert does get in we sit up quite late on very strong gins. I start wondering when he'll say he's going to bed, go comatose and go to sleep. The headache syndrome pisses me off. In bed I moan quite a lot, faking a hell of a lot, being unhappy: emotive blackmail. I ask him what's wrong, is it me, why has he hardly touched me since I went away, all the questions you wanted to ask and never dared. Apparently it's not my fault, something he has to sort out. We leave it at that. He steals the duvet. Shiver. Anyway, it's now Saturday!

I wake very early, about six, then doze again and, after Robert's officially awake – the alarm goes off at 7.30 – exploit my proximity to him. That means that I don't keep my hands to myself. This morning he fucks me. I come over the sheets, three or four massive spurts – wish he could have seen them – with his cock up me, feeling wonderful and warm and very safe at last. A couple of weeks ago he stopped using a condom, which I've appreciated as a sort of recognition that we've been together for a year.

Totter at last to the post; fags and coffee in the front room. Robert's working this morning and won't be back till three. If Dave calls – he didn't last night – I'm to give him Robert's work number. At some point I remember that Robert once said that he'd leave me if Dave, who is straight, were to turn round to him and say he wanted him; and then a few months later Robert said he wouldn't leave me even if that happened.

Saturdays have a rather fixed pattern. First I go off to the flea market, usually quite early, probably calling in to an auction viewing on the way, then the vegetable market and, if Robert's with me, have a couple of pints at the pub. It's difficult to treat Saturdays as unique with this pattern. I wanted to see *Torch Song Trilogy* tonight as a change, but Dave's imminent arrival is unexpected so it will be next week sometime. This Saturday isn't really going to be any different. I go to the flea market looking for another anglepoise lamp, ending up with thirteen coat hooks, a couple of books and a copy of a pre-war AA guide to London for Robert instead of the card I'd still half like to give him. Back home, then out again to buy a ream of paper, vegetables and so on, thinking that since Robert won't be back till three I'll do a couple of hours' work, next week being hairy with a lot of deadlines.

I get back at about one, perhaps a little later since Robert's been back. His cap shines out near the door, keys as well. He's sitting on the sofa and says he has something to tell me. I think

immediately that it's going to be Hepatitis B or AIDS and prepare
to be very supportive and cheerful. It comes out in a rush, after
he hesitates, and then tells me that he's decided to move out, he
has had a word with Suzanne who can put him up, it's not my
fault, he hasn't been feeling right for a couple of months, he
needs to get out and sort things, can we remain friends, will you
promise to say hello to me in the pub sometimes, perhaps not
for ever. I try, at first, to be cheerful, which doesn't work, and
also to be supportive, which I was going to be if it had been
Hep B. Well, I am supportive, hurt as well, but I do want his
life sorted. Being supportive and impeccably fair and so on makes
things worse in a way. I'm being *too* good about it, and probably
love him more than ever. I suppose, then we talk quite a lot. I
cry a lot; he's also crying. Eventually there's little useful to say.
I haven't attempted to change his mind, which I suppose would
be expected of me. He has said he could have killed me when
he saw the AA guide. Talk about number thirteen. That's how
many months we've been together. I realize I've bought thirteen
coat hooks and that I hesitated just before buying them. The
tears, of course, do not stop as long as there is the pain to support
them. I decide that we are going to open the champagne, a black-
humoured celebration. And yes, although I want to say that
there's been a hell of a lot of good in the last thirteen months,
wonderful, lovely things that make me cry as I write this, just
the *thought* of them, I don't say it; we can reminisce later. And,
in a way, I *am* celebrating those thirteen months and also my
own pain and that Robert is at last going to sort himself out.
But should I now be putting my arm around him? How the hell
tonight, in public will I avoid calling him 'darling'? Both mind
and body need retraining.

Halfway into our first glass of champagne, eyes red, wet, the
doorbell rings. I insist on answering it, expecting a window-
cleaner, Jehovah's witness or, at worst, Stewart, another very
boring friend, who can be sent away at once, without compunc-
tion. And, of course, it's two people I've never seen before in
my life, a man and a woman, asking if Robert's in, and I say,
'You must be Dave' and take them upstairs and realize it may
look a little bit odd that we're drinking champagne on a perfectly
ordinary Saturday. Robert's eyes groan, apologizing to me desperately, as he sees us come into the room. It's another cliché,

but I don't know whether to laugh or to cry. Dave and his wife stay for perhaps a couple of hours.

I've changed places in the room and see the wood-engraving on the wall behind the sofa. It's the first thing we got together and it was inscribed to the both of us. At the time we agreed that if we split up then we'd have it cut in half. God, I wish we hadn't agreed that, not because I'm going to hang on to it, I've more than enough pictures and Robert can have it, but because it's a bloody painful memory, which we'll *both* have to confront.

While Dave and his wife are here, Robert keeps up a conversation, confidently flowing. I'm silent, trying hard to look OK and occasionally escaping to bedroom, bog or kitchen to cry or calm down. I start noticing other tangible memories: a scrap of paper tacked up on the bathroom mirror that I did one day as a surprise for Robert when we started going out together. It reads, 'I love you.' In the kitchen, the nineteenth-century ceramic lunch box I gave him exactly a month ago. The telephone, a Christmas present. Me, in a way, because I've learnt masses from him. I cry a lot, privately when Dave and his wife are here. I don't think they've realized aught's amiss, which makes it even more ridiculous when they are going out with Robert tonight, and he'll *have* to tell them.

They leave about three-ish. And we stare at each other, and I can't find many words. There is little to talk about; jokes and the comedy that Dave had to walk right into something awful; and then perhaps we thought we shouldn't be joking like this any more, that we wouldn't be tomorrow, and that doing so today was behaving as if nothing had happened.

There were many apologies, each slightly awkward, but urgent as if we are falling over our own feet to avoid any implication that the other has been in the wrong. It's not how I expected us to break up. I'd thought I'd be much more in the wrong than I am, that the relationship was going to be the problem. I didn't know that it was going to be something that in a way has nothing to do with *us*. I want Robert to know that if he decided to come back, and if I'd done nothing irrevocable meantime, I'd appreciate his reasons for having left. At the moment it occurs to me that we didn't use words like 'breaking up' or 'splitting up'. He just said that he was 'moving out'.

Eventually, much earlier than I'd expected, Robert says he will start packing, if that's all right. I fight tears unsuccessfully, feeling messy. Rational conversation, for having lived together we have accumulations of property. I worry, when Robert packs two bags, whether he's going to take what he needs, whether he's forgetting anything; and hope, and also don't hope, that he'll forget to pack something important. Fuss slightly, trying to make things easier. Don't forget the P45, should you take your files as well now? Say he should keep the keys, it'll make things easier. 'Are you sure?'

The most awkward moment, when he leaves. 'Right, I'll be off now', words to that effect. Ordinary words. I don't know whether I can kiss him. His arm hesitates, rising half-way to touch my shoulder, then he realizes that his body, too, will need retraining, and stops. My hand pats his shoulder, gently. Then I ask if I can help him carry his bags to the car, knowing that it would prolong a parting; and so he goes out of the flat door on to the landing and I think he's gone, and then comes in again to pick up his umbrella; and then I say, 'bye', and he's apologizing and then goes downstairs and I close the door quietly so he won't think I've slammed it after him. And then go into the bedroom and collapse crying, much louder than before, and that's happened, off and on, ever since he left about five hours ago.

After he's left I feel alone. 'Lonely' is a word I never use lightly, and to me it means hideous distress. I break nothing. Don't even really think of killing myself, it would merely be the ultimate blackmail on Robert's heart. I see many things that shout 'us' to me. Objects, thoughts. I attempt to roll a joint, I'd never done it before and really had to concentrate on that. George had borrowed ten quid off me in Edinburgh, and since we'd decided that Robert had to relax and get his mind straight, so why not get him totally pissed and stoned? I said I'd take the repayment as dope. Felt, when I rolled the thing, that perhaps I'd missed the chance by what, thirty-six hours? Wank, viciously, putting a rubber band round my balls, using (Robert's) baby lotion; know that I'm going to depress myself afterwards, which happens. Not very interested in *Vulcan*, and since I'm crying at the time, can't see much anyway. What else? Decide that I don't want to work; think that I'm going to write a diary entry. Try at an accurate description of my feelings, and wish I knew Robert's. And about the first thing I write is:

'Realize that this is the *only* thing I've ever written about Robert; and remember that last year I didn't *dare* put anything down into the diary, full of infatuations and self-loathing. So, as a way of crossing my fingers, I didn't write anything. Wonder a bit later why I'm writing now. At first because I thought that I'd do what I've done at every crisis in my life, I decide to make it interesting. "It was very interesting" covers a multitude of sins.'

While typing I hear a door open or close downstairs. My thoughts change, interpreting today, yesterday, myself. Finally it will be time to eat, then to face Robert, and my own feelings again, in the pub. The penultimate thing was to do a spell-check; I added fuck, fucked, fucks, wank, pissed and P45 to the dictionary.

So, a new relationship with Neil, and the notes on one from which I thought I'd never recover. I do know that I operate best as a couple. And I'm enjoying the renewal of pleasant sensations, the return to life of dead parts of the heart, the challenge of another man's character and the prospect of Sundays at the supermarket, art gallery or in bed.

PETER

I had always hoped for a partner as a companion, lover, an adviser, a confidant, a protector, as someone to kiss goodnight, even as a bulwark against promiscuity. My first, brief partnership was successful for neither of us and lasted, much of it by post, for less than a year. After over forty years with my second it is, I suppose, a marriage without any binding contract, as in a religious or secular marriage contracts are often broken. If we became Danes overnight, I doubt if we would want to sanctify it in public.

We have not been sexually faithful and have each had many transient partners. Our fidelity has never been physical, but spiritual; this was agreed at the outset.

I picked up my partner in my New Zealand home town by the remotest chance. I saw him in the public square late one evening and spoke to him, thinking he was someone who lived locally whom I'd always fancied but did not know. He was there that night, in town after the war, spending his gratuity before settling back into his dull, small-town routine, three hundred miles away. We had sex in his hotel after a short talk. I could never fall in love with anyone, or even contemplate it, before sex has taken place. Attraction may lead to sex but if it is unsatisfactory in any way, and this has happened to me a number of times, friendship may result, but nothing more. Indeed I know of no one with whom I have had unsatisfactory sex that I still see.

My partner and I have adjusted to each other's whims and foibles, not really consciously, for that would be like a constraint, like a contract in a way. Instinctively each knows that certain traits are not liked or approved of by the other. Sex has always been important. I thought once, briefly, that it need not be so important but I was wrong. Now that my partner is seventy-five, and not as demonstrative sexually as he was, I regret it deeply, but it has made no difference to us. Like John Betjeman, 'I haven't had enough sex', and I now only get the rarest of outside offers, I'm sorry to say.

We have had virtually no outside pressures on our relationship. My parents and his had died before we met, and my sister in New Zealand liked him and told him to 'look after' me, but was reputed to have hit the roof many years later when the real relationship was suggested by her husband. Both are now dead but their son is gay and his father knew. A cousin in England is gay and lives openly with his partner; his parents, who are fairly conventional, are completely approving of their relationship and of ours. Other relatives in England, neighbours, colleagues, gay and straight friends always ask each of us how the other is, even after several years' absence; and we have had a joint bank account for over thirty years. A gay bank clerk told us years ago, some time before 1967, that the staff believed that a joint account was a sure sign of a stable couple. We have kissed goodbye in public a few times, but no one has ever commented.

I have been very jealous on three occasions in the past, when my partner was seriously involved with another. I was greatly distressed, grieved, in a way, more than jealous as it did not seem to be making him very happy. But, as he says, I can make him and others feel really guilty merely by my disapproval, rather than by my actions.

When a split did take place and he left me for less than a month, we owned little to divide. Since then, everything has been in common, even a number of sexual partners, so that a divorce is now virtually impossible and so unlikely to raise possession problems. At the time of the split, my successor to his affections suggested that I could be paid off as a form of compensation. When I heard of this, like my sister I too hit the roof. Perhaps it's a family trait. It was not referred to again.

DON

Long-term gay relationships certainly do seem to ape heterosexual marriage. The only long-term gay couple I know certainly behave like this. A is the breadwinner, drives the car, is very bossy, must be obeyed at all times. B is the housewife, does all the cooking and cleaning, is subjugated. I'm sure they will carry on like this, but I know they're both quite unhappy. Real people do not fit these rigid roles.

In gay circles there is still very much a category of people into multi-partnering, heavy cruising, cottaging and the like. I would definitely say that cottaging is increasing in popularity. Of course, with the advent of AIDS, monogamy or celibacy came to the fore as a means of avoiding infection.

I would very much like to see open relationships work, but I am privately cynical about this. There is always one partner who screws around and the other who stays at home and suffers in silence, it seems to me.

I have never had a long-term relationship, but have always wanted one desperately, indeed the lack of one has brought me to the brink of total despair and nervous collapse many, many times in my life. I have never found anyone who wanted me enough. I have tried very hard to make myself attractive, have joined gay groups, have answered and put in lots of lonely hearts advertisements and so on. It may be possible to have a complete and fulfilling life without a long-term lover, but this is not true of me. It is my main ambition to find a long-term lover, certainly to the detriment of my happiness and career. Certainly I have more freedom and privacy as a single person and I think couples envy this in a way. Relationships are a question of compromise after all. Couples like to patronize singles and feel sorry for them, but I think a lot of people who are in relationships feel trapped and stay in them long after they should. I hate the way couples always defend each other and gang up on singles like me.

I'm still longing for it to happen to me. I don't care if I'm aping heterosexuality, I want a relationship!

KEVIN

I am what is normally referred to as a promiscuous gay male. I don't like the word 'promiscuous' because it is overlaid with negative imagery. So let's call it multi-partnering. I seem to need a lot of sex in my life. Without exaggeration I would say that I have probably had sex with as many as three thousand partners in the last twenty-five years or so. This is not a boast, simply a statement of fact. Nor will I apologize for it. Years ago I looked forward to the day when I would share a long-term relationship. I didn't agree with the early theory of the gay liberation lobby which said that long-term relationships aped heterosexual marriage and were therefore to be avoided. I just wanted to need and be needed.

I did have a relationship over some months when I was nineteen. He was a married man about fifteen years older than me. We met in a public lavatory in a northern city and then went to his home. It was Saturday night. His wife was a part-time nurse who worked Saturday nights. I had to leave before she returned. The next week we met up and repeated the events, except that he decided I could sleep the night, but I had to go into a different bed. In the morning he introduced me to his wife as a friend he had met at the theatre and who had missed his last bus. I got on with her and their three daughters, one a little baby, and became a regular weekend visitor, sleeping with him and then moving to the other bed. After a trip to London I discovered I had contracted a venereal disease. He went to the special clinic when he discovered he had caught it from me and wrote me the details of which doctor I should see. I paid my visit to the clinic on the way to staying the weekend. His letter was still in my bag. His wife caught sight of the handwriting and read the letter. She left him, taking the children with her. By that time, the sex had fallen off. I had grown too fond of the wife as a human being and the guilt had got in the way. Our relationship was over. Not long after she went back to him. Years later I returned to the city and looked them up. She had turned into an unpleasant, bitter woman, not the warm friend I had known. He was camper than ever. He now lives in Canada where he had to go to flee the courts, having broken the terms of a suspended sentence for trying to seduce an under-age boy, by doing the same and being found out. Of course, I was under age when he met me though, as it was before 1967, sex between men was totally illegal. We still exchange Christmas cards and the occasional letter.

There have been times when I have continued to have sex with the same person over a number of weeks without any commitment to a relationship. And there have been two or three relationships that I hoped would be long term. There is a theory that sex is better when you're in love. I would say it's different. It's more relaxed because the ground rules are laid down, the likes and dislikes are established, because there is less to prove. One-night-stand sex can, however, be very exciting in a way that a sustained coupling can never be. I feel fortunate that I have experienced both. Until recent years, for the most part every one-night-stand encounter found me thinking, 'Is this going to be the one?' Astrologically, the love planet Venus in my chart is in Aquarius. I once read an interpretation which suggested that people with Venus in Aquarius make more attempts to find their ideal partner! If that isn't a licence for multi-partnering, what could be? I often quote Oscar Hammerstein II and that song from *The King and I*, all that about a man living like a honey bee and gathering all he can. I think that is an innate biological instinct which says that men must spread their seed for the survival of the species. Civilization has inhibited this. Gay liberation liberated it for me.

Because I've met so many men and shared intimacy with them I have had the privilege of insight into many lives. How can I ever forget the Vietnam vet I met in Key West? The sex was pretty good, but all the time I was haunted by the hole in his back. Eventually we relaxed into conversation, naked on the bed, the overhead fan doing nothing to cool us. I asked about the hole and the explanation of his injury led to his memories of that man in the service with whom he had spent many months of combat, while sharing each other's love. He related a foray, the troop moving along a jungle pass. His lover led, he slightly behind. As they moved forward his lover turned and smiled at him, and then his head fell off. He had walked into a wire. I hope I helped that man through that particular night; all that was left of his life seemed to be surviving one night at a time.

I think there is such a thing as love, but I think that most of what is perceived as love at first sight, or even a growing initial love, is a politer way of saying lust. Love, if it exists, is something which stands the test of time and where, perhaps, there is not necessarily a sexual involvement. Jonathan and I met in 1973. He was an American, another Vietnam vet. He had been touring Europe. This was Friday and Sunday he was to fly back home. We were in bed the entire time until he left. We were the same age, the same height, both with moustaches, we could have been brothers. Both of us had some acting experience and had played several parts in common. Star-crossed we certainly seemed to be. Indeed we had a romantic notion that we could send messages by saying 'hello' to the stars. He came back to England again in 1977. I had moved but somehow he managed to track me down. He finally traced me on the Friday when he was due to leave on the Sunday. History repeated itself; we were in bed the whole weekend. Back in the States, he found some way of phoning me at a pre-arranged public telephone box and charging the calls to some large, unscrupulous multinational company and we talked long into the night. It wasn't his idea, numerous people were doing it and eventually the system was changed.

In 1980 I made my first trip to New York. Jonathan was in a relationship and I stayed with him and his lover. He said we would find some time to make love but we didn't that time or on subsequent visits. Every time I went to New York, he would receive my first telephone call. We always met. The first meeting each trip, and the last, would be marked by the most passionate, lingering hug. It seemed to go on so long that I would get almost embarrassed by it, then give into it. We would eat together and go to the theatre. The former lover is now dead. But I met Jonathan's subsequent lover, also called Jonathan, and we became friends. The last time I saw Jonathan was in 1987 when a mutual friend asked how long we had known one another. I said it had been fourteen years. He couldn't believe it. One time he almost died, something to do with his brain, I never did understand quite what it was. I was in New York at the time. I think that was the first time that I told him that not only did I love him, but that I was in love with him. He said he felt the same.

The two Jonathans eventually moved to Hawaii to escape the never-ending procession to the crematorium of all their friends and spend their last years together in the sun in a beautiful place. I knew I would probably never see him again as it would have been impossible for me to afford the journey. I was right. A letter arrived from the other Jonathan to tell me that 'our brave and noble friend' had died. He had developed full-blown AIDS five months earlier.

I had said to Jonathan that he was the continuity in my life. Now that's gone, without any goodbye. He will always be a part of me; the stars are always there. His framed photograph, as he was when we first met, hangs on the wall and I still check with him as *my* life moves on. At least his head doesn't fall off in my memory. There it remains, the smile of his eyes and he, on the brink of life.

SCOTT

I have never had a long-term, live-in relationship. I have had lovers and boyfriends, some of whom are still friends. I am not in touch with any former girlfriends, though I do have some close friendships with women. Chances are that I may soon be setting up home with someone.

I do not see any point in multiple casual coupling. That sort of behaviour bored me in the days before AIDS was heard of. Being bisexual I could never settle into 100 per cent monogamy. A likely scenario is a sort of quasi-'open' relationship. I would settle down with a live-in partner, preferably him or herself bisexual, and we would allow each other a margin of privacy in which to have a subsidiary affair. Whether we could make these subsidiary affairs lasting, or have a string of secondary lovers, I do not know.

People are different. I should not like to criticize them just for having different needs to mine. When gay couples are criticized for aping heterosexual marriage, all I can say is that there are different models of heterosexual marriage. 'Conventional' marriages come in almost as many shapes and sizes as 'unconventional' ones.

I live alone in this two-room flat. I have got it arranged and furnished the way I like it. I rather like the way I live, even if I sometimes feel lonely. I cope with this loneliness, and the conviction that I shall not always be on my own is only one of the devices by which I cope. If still alone in old age or, for that matter, if I outlive a long-term partner, I feel sure I will come through it.

CHRISTOPHER

We started seeing each other on a regular basis, first as friends and then as something more. It was usually every other weekend and some weekday evenings. He lived outside the city and commuted into work. We would take a hotel room as I was still living with my parents, have a meal or see a show on the Friday, with a disco afterwards and a gallery or museum next day. I usually saw him off at the railway station, always feeling very depressed. I think I shed a tear on more than one occasion. It was eventually obvious to both of us that we felt more than friendship for each other; we were emotionally close and had interests in common, the makings of a good affair. I remember the evening we decided to live together; we were sitting in a burger bar and each, more or less simultaneously, asked the other how he felt about living together. This was a big step for me as I had never lived away from home before, despite being in my late twenties. On the other hand, Nigel, who was some nine years older than me, owned a house in the town where he lived, to which we would temporarily move until we were both sure we wanted to live together and, assuming that was the case, could find a place together.

The biggest problem as far as I was concerned was that I knew my mother would disapprove. Before I met Nigel I had been considering moving to a flat of my own and that upset her. She couldn't understand why I would want to give up the advantages of home living and having my cooking and cleaning done for me. I knew there would be emotional scenes which I find difficult to face. It did not help that she didn't like Nigel when she first met him. She caught us kissing in the front room. It was childish of me and a selfish thing to do, but I suppose I wanted the same rights my sister had when she brought a boyfriend home. Anyway, she thought he was a trouble-maker and thought I should see less of him.

I must admit I was a bit of a coward about telling her I was leaving; rather than tell her face to face I left a note when I set off for work one morning. As a result I got a rather tearful phone call at work. When I refused to change my mind, despite repeated blandishments, she came to accept the situation.

After the hassle of moving at least some of my possessions to Nigel's house, I was surprised how quickly I settled in and how little I felt homesick. I found household chores easy and got a routine going. For example I did the washing most; he, as he was usually in first in the evening, did the cooking; we shared the shopping. It was all new and exciting. However, one basic problem arose right at the beginning – sex. Before I moved in with Nigel we had a fairly active sex life, and I hoped that for a year or two when we first lived together I could remain monogamous, a relief from the continual search for sex on the scene. I had the impression that he wanted to do the same; however, as soon as I moved in, Nigel no longer wanted sex. Nothing was said, and in other ways he was still affectionate, but he ignored my advances. I didn't feel I could bring the subject up because when we had first met I had said that sex wasn't everything in a relationship, and other things were just as important so that to bring it up now made me seem to be a hypocrite. I must admit I was devastated at first; I thought he didn't love me any more, that I had done something to upset him. My fine resolutions about monogamy were going to need revision. I'm a fairly sexual person, and did not feel able to undertake celibacy in order to remain faithful. At the same time I still cared for Nigel. As in every other way it was still a good relationship I decided to keep it going to see how things worked out. Eventually I realized that it was a desire for companionship rather than sex on Nigel's part which had caused this situation. Bar one occasion, the situation never changed in the three years I lived with him.

The inevitable happened of course and I started having sex outside the relationship. Illogically I felt guilty to begin with even though the situation was not of my making. Most of these encounters were in cottages and anonymous, so I didn't feel compelled to tell Nigel. However, one night when he was away for the weekend I met a very sexy young guy at the disco. He lived with his parents so we couldn't go back to his place. I said I would arrange a hotel for the following evening, arranging to meet up with him in a nearby pub. During the day I did some household chores feeling very guilty, both hoping he would and would not turn up. The lie pained me more than the prospective sex. I am a Buddhist by religion and truthfulness is something I have always striven for. Anyway, he was there at the pub and we spent a most enjoyable night. Afterwards, I felt I ought to tell Nigel. He took it in good part, treating it as a joke. This took a weight off my mind as it meant he had no objections to me having outside sex. If he was away weekends from then on I would feel free to meet other men.

As the years went by I was fairly happy and I think Nigel was too. We shared a sense of humour, we shared interests and we visited places together. Occasional arguments were soon made up. However, he was prone to moodiness. Sometimes the pressure of his work got too much for him and he got very depressed. This was made manifest in his being uncommunicative and withdrawn, or he would berate the people he worked with. Nothing I said would soothe him and I would have to wait until his mood changed. Living where we did I felt isolated from my friends and cut off from the cultural life I had got used to. None of this, in itself, would have caused me to leave as I wasn't desperately unhappy, but the seeds of dissatisfaction had been planted. Then last year, just before a holiday in Thailand, I spent a week in Amsterdam visiting a friend. Nigel had also gone on holiday; it was our first separate holiday. The first evening I was there I got chatting to another guy staying at the same hotel. We got on well together and shared some common interests, in particular a sincere belief in Buddhism, so I arranged to meet him later. It was one of my best evenings ever; we talked and made love till 2 am, but neither of us noticed the time. I spent most of the weekend with the friend I had come to visit but bumped into Mick at breakfast the morning I was due to go home, and agreed to meet him later that day. The same sense of compatibility was there and I knew that feelings of more than friendship were developing. What should I do? Was this just a holiday romance or something more serious? Luckily I had an opportunity to find out.

Nigel was still away when I got back, so I saw Mick several times before going to Thailand, and the feelings were still there on my home turf. However, any decision had to be put off till I got back from Thailand when I resolved to tell Nigel the situation. But this plan backfired because, on my return, Nigel was down with a serious viral infection picked up on his return from holiday. He was badly ill, and I even had to take time off work to look after him, as he could do nothing for himself he was so weak. It was obviously out of the question to tell him of my dilemma; it would have been like kicking him when he was down. However, my frustration began to mount, particularly when he said how glad he was that I was there, and what would he do without me. I felt an absolute heel; I was living a lie, and not being fair to him or Mick. The longer I left it I knew the harder it would be to tell Nigel as I have never had much courage in telling people unpleasant truths. However, when Nigel was on his way to recovery he asked me if anything was wrong as I hadn't seemed my old self since I had returned from holiday. Given this golden opportunity I took my courage in both hands and told him everything. He was shaken, though not entirely surprised as I had mentioned Mick several times in glowing terms. He said that whatever I decided he wanted to remain my friend as true friends were difficult to find; with this I whole-heartedly agree.

As the weeks went by I gradually found the strength to make a decision, and decided on Mick. Nigel said that on no account was I to move back to my parents in the interim as this would cause unnecessary complications and encourage my mother to try to get me to move back permanently. I stayed at Nigel's during the week and stayed most weekends with Mick. In this way I got to know him in a domestic situation, while not having too quick a break from Nigel, a gradual transition. All our friends accepted the split, though were naturally concerned. My mother, on the other hand, got rather upset. She had grown to like Nigel, and possibly thought I was being unfair to him, an echo, perhaps, of being left by my father for a time when I was young.

Mick and I started looking for a flat and found one we liked and could afford almost immediately. We are very happy together, both because we have each other and because the cultural life of the city is at our feet. One strength of our relationship is that neither of us is jealous by nature, so we have a fairly open relationship. The only rules are that no strange 'trade' is brought back to the flat, and if we go out together neither picks up a third party, and we go home together. In this way our home life and social life together is protected from possible tensions, and our property is protected from possible theft. Other than that, sexual liaisons are quite accepted; we love each other enough to know the difference between physical and emotional fidelity and that insistence on the first could put the second at risk.

Another strength of our relationship is our shared religion. This allows us to see our relationship as a growing thing which changes with time, rather than as a once and for all thing, and an area where personal growth can occur. I lacked this sense of personal growth with Nigel, and this as much as the other things I mentioned helped undermine the relationship; a certain depth was missing.

NICK

The experience of love, no matter how short, is what I prayed to God for. I was in my early twenties. Of course, I would have preferred a long-term relationship but God allowed me only a brief one which ended bitterly.

I met Gary at a CHE meeting to which I had been taken by a befriender. He took me back to my home in his car and I experienced my first man-to-man kiss. He did not actually physically attract me but I so desperately wanted a relationship that I forced myself into what I thought was love. We moved in together and started to do everything together.

My only sexual activity before meeting him had been solitary, fetishist and compulsive. When we attempted sex together I failed miserably. This upset us both, of course. I made things worse by harping on about previous close, albeit platonic, relationships.

I discovered what a foreskin was and that mine could not be drawn back so it was arranged for me to be circumcised both for medical reasons and because I hoped it would make me more sexually responsive to Gary. As a result of the operation I went through several weeks of sexual abstinence and when at last I approached him to renew our sex life I was rebuffed. He started to bring sex partners home. We went to the same social events but he went with his new lovers and I felt publicly humiliated. After a few months I moved out.

Later, I met a man and became friendly with him but did not have sex at first, preferring to establish a relationship first. We went to a party together but I left alone. He left with Gary.

Since then, nothing. My sexual incompetence, my jealousy, my humiliation and my parents' suspicion have kept me unhappily celibate for eleven years. Still, I probably haven't been infected by AIDS. But I do wonder from time to time about a lonely and helpless old age.

RICHARD

John and I were together for just over three years when the relationship ended in his death. After that there was Naveed who lasted a year and was a borderline case. With hindsight there was an element of rebound following John's death so I'm not going to describe that liaison further. Much more recently there has been Marius, who I am with at the moment.

I met John in South London where we both lived. We had seen each other in the area and knew each other by name. He first chatted me up in the Clapham Road Sainsburys where he had followed me for precisely that purpose. I suppose it says something for the other places he might have chosen that he made his approach in a supermarket since we used many of the same pubs, clubs and cafes. I'd never had a strong emotional relationship before, and I include my parents in this, and at first there seemed something rather ridiculous about the situation. I suppose I was so lacking in self-confidence that the moment someone expressed interest in me as a person rather than just as a sexual partner, my first action was to question his sense of judgement!

Marius, by contrast, I first met at the house of a friend with whom he had recently started a relationship so that's one person who isn't a friend any more! That was much more of a mutual initiative. I had been invited round to meet Marius; we just happened to get on really well and I asked for a date.

I think that at the start of every relationship there's a Lover and a Beloved. The ones that last are the ones where this gives way to a more equal pattern. With Marius I was the one who started out as the Lover, whereas with John it was the other way around.

How this process of adjustment takes place I am not quite sure. It's something you don't know has taken place until afterwards. At first John was much more interested in me than I was with him. Because we lived near each other anyway, once I'd got into a regular sexual relationship with him, and there was a commitment in my doing that, I soon discovered that he was precisely what had been missing from my life. The imbalance with Marius, on the other hand, stopped when he broke off with my former friend and began arranging his life to fit in with mine. Up to then I'd been the Lover.

John, because of his interest in my body, stimulated my own and thanks to him I started taking much more of an interest in clothes, in what I ate, working out and so on. There were always differences and disagreements. John never smoked and neither does Marius, and they both discouraged me because of their worries about my health. But I've never even tried giving up. There's one particular disagreement I'd like to describe because of what it says about my relationship with John. Soon after we set up house together I decided I wanted us to have a cat. I've always loved cats but John didn't like animals – 'Who's going to feed it when we're away?' Well, I teased him that he was jealous, he insisted that he wasn't and I left it at that. I thought that was the end of it, only on my birthday he bought me a kitten. Now the point is, if I'd made a scene, making a point every time we visited anyone with a cat and the like, he'd not have done it. I had signalled that I didn't think it was important enough to push for beyond making my feelings clear, and he responded when he realized how much it meant to me, and that he could submit without feeling he'd been manipulated into doing so.

What I give up most for Marius right now is time. We don't live together and if I feel he needs me I'll drop other arrangements for him. I get very annoyed when people criticize me for this. Before Marius I was alone for quite a long time, and I got used to being able to change my mind whenever it suited me. I might get half way to a theatre of an evening and then decide I didn't really want to see the play and just go home. I don't do that any more. But we still do impulsive, subversive things together that I would never have dreamed of doing alone or with an ordinary friend. The most memorable is playing 'I Spy' on a crowded tube train.

Sex is important in my relationships and, though I've always considered myself to have a relatively low sex drive, the only way into my life is through my bed. I've found it becomes less important as the relationship progresses, but not that much less. I really don't know if, say, there was some reason why Marius and I could not have sex together again, the relationship would last. I rather doubt it. As far as frequency is concerned, as I said, I have a relatively low sex drive. John was very sensitive about this, but then he knew that soon after I'd started going out with him I had been sexually assaulted. As a man I hesitate to use the word 'rape' but it was certainly sex without my consent. I've never told Marius this, and I certainly find myself occasionally pretending a desire I don't feel. It's complicated by the fact that his work takes him out of London a lot so when he comes back early after a week in Scotland obviously he isn't inclined to listen to any 'not tonights'. With John I was more keen on the idea of group sex than he was and I never pushed it, although he said he wouldn't have minded if I'd done it without involving him. When the safer sex guidelines were first being promulgated I insisted we learn to use condoms. Marius had had sex with women before he came out but I'd never seen a condom before. I found them offputting and we have an undertanding not to fuck with anyone else.

We've had conflict over outside pressures because I am very open about myself and Marius less so. Not so much over parents. Mine are divorced; I don't have anything to do with my mother, and my father lives at the other end of the country, though I'm out to them both. His parents live abroad and are Catholics and he is afraid of being rejected by them. I hope his views on this will change, and I think they've worked out everything there is to know anyway. We had a successful Christmas with my father last year. I don't think there were any problems with John's parents until he died when they became very proprietorial about his body and his possessions. It got very ugly and none of us were in a state to react like rational human beings. I realize that for those three years I had been tolerated for his sake rather than accepted as part of the family.

After his death and the one not very successful relationship soon after, I lived alone for several years. Once you learn to make the distinction between loneliness and solitude there's a value in that sort of independence and I think I'd find it difficult now to live with someone I was having a relationship with. That's because there are now times I have to be alone, and it's difficult for someone else to realize that that does not constitute rejection of them. At present things are OK with Marius but we may have to come to a decision on this in the next twelve months.

The green-eyed god is a part of human nature and there's nothing wrong with jealousy so long as you recognize it for what it is and that it comes from within yourself. I was jealous of John's relationship with his parents until I realized that it was because my relationship with my own had been so impoverished. The problem with jealousy is that it makes you do such petty things that you're ashamed of afterwards. John was quite keen on opera, and one birthday someone I was jealous of gave him a recording of *Carmen* which I deliberately played so carelessly that it got scratched. I'm still ashamed of that to this day and my penance is that I can't hear 'L'amour est un oiseau rebelle' ('Love is a rebellious bird') without thinking of it. Quite an apt aria under the circumstances.

Divorce hasn't arisen because John died. It was a total surprise, a car accident, and as his parents did not live in London I had to identify the body. The inquest was one of the worst experiences of my life. To the police and everyone else John was just a fatality whereas to me he was the most important person in my life. All they wanted to establish was that I'd known him long enough to be able to identify him. I felt it was a denial of all we ever had together to let it go like that. I kept thinking, if only we had been married then I could have shown my grief. My friends didn't know how to react, I don't think any of them had lost a lover. There was nobody to turn to. The Gay Bereavement Project didn't then exist, or I hadn't heard of it if it did, and I couldn't go to a counsellor and have to explain the whole thing from scratch and risk being totally rejected. I've never felt so vulnerable before or since. On top of that his parents, who had always seemed very accepting towards me, took over all the arrangements for the funeral. He had died intestate and they expected to have all his things, though they could only have sold them. My advice to anyone in a relationship reading this is please, please make joint wills. You'll save so much trouble. It rather surprised Marius that I brought up the subject so soon in our relationship but he understands why. I realize that John's parents must have been devastated at losing their only son, but in other circumstances we could have helped each other through it.

PHILIP

Until I was fifty-five I had never experienced or felt the need of a long-term relationship. This is with the single exception of one year in my early forties when I saw one man about once a week. The rest of my life was a continuum of one-off encounters, with the occasional repeat with the same partner from time to time, but no attachments. That was until 1980 when I met Bob, and then Hugh. Basically they are both bisexual, Bob with less experience, Hugh with a good deal. Bob is the one I grew attached to and came to love. But our meetings are not often more frequent than once every two or three weeks or even longer. Hugh is a more frequent visitor. They are both married and live with their wives. Both are a year older than I.

I met them both in the same place, a popular cruising area on the nearby beach, Bob in the day time, Hugh at night. Bob and Hugh have never met, incidentally, but they know of each other's existence. I have explained to Hugh that Bob is my first priority and Bob knows that Hugh calls here. Hugh and I have never *slept* together, we have an evening session and then he goes home. With Bob there have been the rare occasions when his wife has been away and I have stayed with him one or two nights. And we have had a short mid-week holiday break at a seaside resort.

As our backgrounds are so very different we have little in common apart from sex. My interests tend to the studious and cultural whereas Bob is no reader and follows sport closely, as does Hugh. In the early years Hugh used to be very pushy as regards sex when he wanted it. He would never take 'no' for an answer, but went on and on. Gradually he has modified his pressuring and accepts it unquestioningly when I say it is not convenient, or I do not feel like it, or that Bob has been or is expected. So we get to have sex about once a week. I never refuse Bob, but these days am not always up to a good performance with him, although I rarely fail to come satisfactorily with Hugh. This is a bit of a mystery to me as I regard Bob as my lover, and Hugh as the second string. It may lie partly in Bob's less experienced love-making. He rarely attempts to caress me other than kissing and occasional sucking, wheras Hugh will go further and stroke and stimulate my nipples and so on. I've never had any sexual activity which I haven't enjoyed, but then I've always been my own man. If I didn't wish to drink, and I'm no great drinker, then I would not be coerced or cajoled into drinking. The same with sex.

BRUCE

I suppose that, other than for a relatively short period of my life, altogether not more than three years, I have had a succession, essentially, of long-term relationships. The present one has lasted now over thirteen years and still continues to be wonderful, and

I am seventy this year and my partner three years my senior. However, we do not live together although we spend as many as four nights a week together. This relationship started through an advertisement I placed in the old *Gay News*. I have never been clubbable or pubbable, nor much group-minded. The advert was not a sexual one, but seeking to meet another in the same area who had certain qualities. Without either of us having such an intention in meeting we had sex the first night we met. With almost all my relationships, other than in my promiscuous spell of three years, I have always looked for friendship initially, rather than sex.

I don't think I have *had* to change to accommodate my partner, although I have, in fact, changed a great deal. I cannot think of any changes I have sought of him. I have stopped smoking, have become almost vegetarian and have developed a taste, as has he, for avant garde cinema and ballet. I do sometimes behave quite irrationally towards him, for perhaps a week or so, at intervals of months or even years, when I seem totally to lose sight of how very dear he is to me and how much I love him, and feel quite incredulous about my relationship with him and be quite angry with him and myself that I am involved in a situation that at the time seems to me to be quite absurd in the extreme. Then, overnight, the phase will end so that I am back with him fully and as appreciative of him as ever I was. It's quite alarming and neither of us can find any explanation for it. It is only I who have these spells, my partner never but, he says, he puts up with them because by now he feels that they will be transitory, and that they are some kind of reaction by me against the tying effect of a monogamous relationship and because, at the end of the day, these spells seem to strengthen rather than weaken our relationship.

Sex remains very important to our relationship, no less now than throughout. There is never a period of more than a couple of hours when we are together where there is not some manifestation of our sexual attraction to each other. We still have sex at least once a day when we are together, and quite often more than once. I can't ever remember a time when either of us has rejected the sexual overtures of the other. Any sexual activity we have is always mutually agreeable between us.

Very recently, in my partner's quite long absence abroad, I have become involved, though not yet sexually, with someone decades younger than myself. My partner knows and accepts this. I find it exhilarating and, at the same time, *very, very, very* frightening to be involved to the extent I am in this after all these years exclusively with my partner.

TOM

I spent my teenage years and early adulthood in putting on an act. I pretended to be normal, went out with and had sex with girls, while longing for my next secretive visit to the toilet in the park and Soho where I could have sexual pleasure with men. I recall when I first met gay men in bars and pubs it was marvellous. Open, fun, outrageous – and a bit scary, but very exciting. The images presented to me at the time were of gay men playing parts. Some were active, others were passive, just like men and women. If you were labelled 'butch' you were expected to be the boyfriend or the husband in the relationship. Likewise if you were the passive partner you were seen as the girlfriend or wife. It's interesting that if you were classified as 'butch' you had a better standing in the group; if passive, like women in general you had less standing, you had to be submissive to the 'butch'. More negative images to model myself on. Society saw me as a female substitute and the gay community at that time led me to my own self-oppression by pretending to be heterosexuals, even in the relationships they made with other gay men. However, I must add that in my youth and early adulthood I had lots of fun, was well supported and wouldn't have missed it. It had everything wrong with it, but we made something of it, and it was all right.

My first learning about positive images was when gay liberation started. This changed all my perceptions about myself. It was breathtaking. Suddenly we were unwilling to disguise and act straight. The language changed, debates raged and I felt good. I realized that all the years before, especially the ones with Derek, had been of the highest value. We had been good people, oppressed without knowing it, getting unjust desserts and not deserving it. It was a good time and we became involved, visible and out.

My main fears when in the closet were the fear and panic of being found out. I knew of friends who had spent long periods in prison because they had been caught or because, in some police investigation, their address books had been seized. The sense of living on a knife's edge was a constant one.

The experience of liberation was so different from what went before. No more going to the doctor for a 'cure', no more pretence. I was thirty-seven at the time. Derek and I had been together for twelve years. Neither side of the families had been told of the real nature of our relationship. We had always been good mates who lived together. Both my parents and Derek's mum died before we came out. I think they would have understood; they were good parents.

In all Derek and I were together for twenty-nine-and-a-half years.

I was twenty-five, it was 1962. I was just completing my service in the Royal Navy, still had a few months to serve and had rented a small courtyard flat in Plymouth in readiness for my return to civvy street. In my youth before joining the Navy I had had many infatuations which, when reciprocated, remain as jewels in my memory. Life for queers in the 1950s was cosy, hectic and lots of fun, but the idea of setting up a home together was fraught with difficulties. Some who lived in the anonymous zones of the bedsits did sometimes manage to build relationships based on shared space. For others on the outskirts of London who still lived with their parents, they had to watch their 'p's and q's'. I was like the rest. Anyone I felt pangs for at the time was purely a dating partner, someone I would have sex with on someone else's bed or in dark passageways and discreet gardens in the West End of London.

This changed when I joined the Royal Navy in 1957 with my friend Neil. We joined specifically for the rum, bum and baccy. And found it in abundance. It was five years of my life in which I was totally fulfilled. I made many friends and learned much about the secret and discreet ways of gay living in many ports, realizing the universality of gayness. It was everywhere, it was part of the natural order of things.

Well, as I said earlier, I was now due to leave the Navy. I had been based in Plymouth for the last year of my service. During this time I had developed a network of friends, knew where the gay pub was and had had time to find out where the best cottages were. I was set for civvy street with a job to go to. Then I met Derek. He was waiting with a friend for their last bus and I was wandering back home alone. He was eighteen and so beautiful.

I stopped to admire this stranger from a distance. As in all the romantic song lyrics our eyes met and we passed signals of desire. I don't know to this day how he managed to get his companion on to the bus and managed to miss it himself and share the night with me.

We lived through all the pressures of waiting to be together. We made a home, had friends, learned how to be ourselves, lots of ups and downs, but despite the tugs and pulls of gay hedonism and disguising from family the truth of our relationship, we survived. We moved to London pursuing our careers. The gay community was inbred and frequently self-destructive in its relationships. Derek and I were like the rest, into playing hetero-sexual role models of him and her, husband and wife: the one that was always fucked and the one that did the fucking. This proved difficult for me because I had always liked to play both active and passive roles and enjoyed both. Now I was in a relationship where I was always expected to play the man. That's what happened with Derek and I had to go elsewhere to meet the other objects of my sexual desires. This double life within a double life of living as straight was common practice at the time. But Derek was special and the person I wanted to come home to and be together with. The conflicts imposed of our innocent self-oppression through the pressures to conform to inappropriate role models was less important than our being together.

Our world began to fall apart when the pressures became too great and we both took solace in the bottle. It was a turbulent time, both of us continuing to work, but the wanting to be together leading to discord. We had enough strength left in the relationship to know that the problem was exacerbated by drinking and we both stopped. We came together again, the relationship more loving, each negotiating space for the other. Although not without its problems, this was a wonderful part of our being together.

The great test of our strength in one another, however, was the arrival of HIV, and the arrival of friends and others wanting help. We both worked hard to establish a local contact group for people with HIV and AIDS. This fully reunited us. It was some-thing only two lovers could have accomplished because it grew out of the love we had for one another. It put into perspective who we were and what we meant to each other. Neither Derek nor I knew our HIV status at the time, but were both busy extolling safer sex as the ultimate answer to the spread of HIV. When Derek began to look unwell, the doctor said it was an ulcer. We continued to work hard at the project and then he developed PCP and Kaposi's Sarcoma. I didn't believe it; we had been careful for as long as we had known about HIV. Derek was admitted to hospital and struggled for his life; he didn't want to die. He survived this episode and returned to work, played and won a tennis tournament and saw the opening of our project's centre, celebrated Christmas and his forty-seventh birthday on 30 December 1989, the New Year's Eve fund-raising party, and died at 3.30 pm on Tuesday 2 January 1990.

Since then I have been more alone than at any time in my life. I find it difficult to adjust to his not being here. Having him to laugh with, disagree with, just being together. I miss the honesty of his responses and now begin to doubt my own. I am aware of the silence that has descended upon me.

7

Virus

KEVIN

I remember one evening I was travelling to spend some time with a new friend. Sitting opposite me was a pimply, unattractive youth and at the other end of the tube carriage was a gaggle of girls. He couldn't take his eyes off them. I had been studying him for several minutes, the desperation of lust for the girls and the hopelessness of it all when, suddenly, he saw me. A look of utter contempt coloured his face. I turned away, amused that he thought I was eyeing him up; nothing could be further from the truth. There was I with an evening promising dinner and good sex, and there was he going nowhere. I think it was then it first occurred to me that a backlash against gays was inevitable. We were having it too good for them. There's an often repeated joke about the 1960s that no one knows anyone who was actually there when what the 1960s is legendary for was happening. In the 1970s it was happening too, and gay men were exclusively in on the action. We had rejected heterosexual standards and made our own rules, finding the sexual freedoms which were the envy of all. No wonder, when HIV came along, that many saw it as a punishment; they couldn't have wished a more effective retribution.

What is unforgivable is the perception that gay men have *wilfully* spread the virus. This is mainly ignorance about the way it works. The incubation period is long. Many people who are becoming ill now may have been infected long before anyone knew of its existence.

In the spring of 1983 a call went out through the gay press for volunteers to have their sex lives monitored in case it would throw any light on the transmission of HTLVIII, as it was then known. I went along. We were given blood tests and asked to fill out a questionnaire, and this was repeated every few months. Each time we would complete a sex diary of the previous few weeks. We were also given information on what were thought, at that time, to be the practices to avoid. From then on I have practised safer sex. At that time there was no test. That came in during 1984 and all the blood samples we gave that month were automatically screened. Mine was found to be positive. This meant that I had been infected before 1983. It is most likely that it had happened as long ago as 1980 when the virus was travelling about unrecognized.

It would never happen today, but I was given no counselling. This would have been available but I had insisted on being notified by post. Consequently, I had to deal with it alone. In fact I didn't have HIV counselling for another six years, followed by bereavement counselling in 1991. I have always said that HIV has robbed me of ambition. Initially, I expected to be dead within six months. This meant I couldn't plan beyond, and this expectation lasted the first three or four years. I began to drink heavily, but saw the error of that, fortunately. I went back to teaching for a time. Focusing on the futures of others was a positive step. Now, I have cautiously welcomed back ambition and undertake projects which need the passage of time to bring to completion.

Throughout I have been involved with drugs trials because I have always felt it important to be doing something about the virus. I have avoided situations which might cause me stress. Thinking of the seventy or more friends and acquaintances who have died, the majority have been people who led very stressful lives. There are periods of chronic exhaustion when I can't work, so there's seldom very much in my bank account. The gay scene has done virtually nothing to accommodate people in this situation in concessions and reduced entry to clubs and so on.

My T-cell count plunged dramatically after the death of Jonathan and it looked as though AIDS was finally here, but I'm still here and I'm still the same as I've been all these seven years. I don't worry about symptoms any more, or check myself for KS lesions as I did every day for years. When I began attending a different clinic my new doctor said, 'Are you still having sex?' 'Yes,' I said. 'Good,' said he. It's more intermittent these days, but my appetites may well have diminished with age anyway.

Many partners are HIV positive too, others are not. It doesn't matter either way; no one puts anyone at risk.

The crisis has produced heroes: Elizabeth Taylor, for one, who stood up and was counted before it became fashionable. And that simple, single act that told the world there was nothing to worry about, when the Princess of Wales went against all previous protocol and wore no gloves the day she visited an AIDS hospice, shaking hands with every patient. I am moved by that every time I think of it. Rather than be the irresponsible perpetrators of the epidemic, as has been the characterization by the ignorant to the ignorant, gay men have taken responsibility, both in example and in providing care, for the community at large.

The following passages were all written early in 1986

KEITH

The way I feel about AIDS is similar to the way I feel about cancer: I only think about it when the subject is raised or I read about it. Of course I have thought about it but, as the saying goes, life has to go on, and there are so many distractions in this world that are designed to take your mind off death, that eventually you just think of things such as AIDS when you are confronted by the thing, or personally affected by it. Yes, it does scare me, because it's not a thing I can ignore because it is something that can kill me, but it is not a perpetual fear, just one that crops up now and again when the subject is brought up.

You talk about the AIDS crisis. What do you mean by this? Well, it hasn't infringed on my lifestyle. Yes, I do know about the safe-sex guidelines, and do try to implement them as a part of my sexual activity, but, like a lot of gay men, sex to me is very spontaneous and therefore cannot really be prepared for. As for finding it difficult to give up sexual activities, can I ask you a question? Would a person find it difficult to give up breathing?

IAN

Yes, the health crisis has changed my lifestyle. I have become aware of the safer-sex guidelines over the past year or two. Until a couple of days ago I had not fucked for about two years even with my regular boyfriend. We have discussed AIDS and agreed to 'be sensible', safe sex only, even between ourselves. Two days ago I fucked using a condom for the first time in my life. A man I picked up wanted it and he provided the condom. Now I will buy some in case such a situation recurs and the other guy has not got a sheath. I have picked up fewer people than I would have done had it not been for AIDS, for about the past two years. But every month has made me more concerned and aware.

I have not had the HTLVIII test and until a week or two ago was fairly sure I didn't want it; now I'm less sure, having talked to several friends who have and to a doctor at an AIDS meeting who told me that there is a *medical* advantage in finding out as early as possible that one is positive. The test has only been available in this city for a couple of months, so the problem of 'to test or not to test' has not been an immediate one until now. This, in itself, horrified a friend from London when I told him about a local friend who recently found out he was positive and who has not been following the safe-sex guidelines but screwing around a lot. When they found out he was positive they tested blood taken at a previous ordinary check-up ten months ago and found that that too was positive, since when he has had many partners on trips here and abroad. 'For God's sake,' asked my London friend, 'why didn't they test for HTLVIII back then?' 'Because the test wasn't available here until two months ago,' I told him. If he had lived in London he would have known much earlier and probably have had fewer, if any, sex partners.

Personally, of course I am afraid of AIDS. Not terrified; occasionally complacent − 'after all, only a couple of hundred out of fifty million have developed it' − other times, quite scared − '90 per cent of gay men in Los Angeles are now supposed to be HTLVIII positive, how long before that's so here too?'. . . .

RICHARD

AIDS does not scare me because I am well informed about it. I think about it and its effects a lot and also about the way it is treated in the media. Friends from the provinces often ask me if AIDS has affected gay morality − not that I like the phrase. I don't think it has affected gay lifestyles as much as it should. Someone recently dismissed the AIDS crisis to me because 'I don't know anyone with AIDS', this from an involved member of the gay community. It seems awful that people have to wait until the crisis impinges on their personal life to even begin to think about it. But then it impinged on mine at an early stage, having lost a friend to an AIDS-related disease. I know about the safe-sex guidelines but I find my intermittent reading of the medical literature casts doubt on any firm assertions about the transmission of AIDS. I am careful with my lover because I care about him more than about myself, although at other times I do let myself go and then worry about it afterwards because, of course, that is precisely the sort of occasion when you should consider safe sex.

I have not taken the test and, in view of the absence of any treatment at present, don't see the point in doing so. I asked myself what conclusions I could make from the test. Answer, none. If I'm positive for the antibody I might develop ARC or AIDS or I might not; if I do take the test with a negative result, I should take it again after every sexual activity.

AIDS has, to a large extent, turned the gay male community in on itself at a time when some of us have been trying to build bridges with other types of social oppression and control – racial, sexual, class – and that's a pity. On the other hand, it has emphasized the fact that the situations of lesbians and of gay men are very different, something we sometimes try to hide under a veneer of gay solidarity.

Just when even the most bigoted straights are realizing that 'queen' jokes are losing their credibility, now we have the AIDS jokes, which are far more damaging and hurtful. You can tell a lot about people's greatest anxieties by their jokes.

STEPHEN

One feels a duty to say something profound about AIDS, but others have said enough and in my own life AIDS isn't much of a worry. I worry about it generally because of how society reacts to gay men *en bloc* – and, however pedantic we wish to be, the HTLVIII virus is one which is primarily transmitted by gays – and because I see gays as, in a sense, a community, members of which are dying, that has to be disturbing. Personally, though, it doesn't worry me; it's a disease which affects others, not myself. And whenever I have sex it's very safe.

In a way AIDS has been a good thing, or rather it has had

some beneficial effects. I mean that it changes other people's lifestyles, and consequently what they expect of me as a sexual partner, if indeed they want sex at all. The people I've slept with were quite happy just with mutual masturbation. My impression is that sex has less part to play in the lives of gay people, those that I know that is. I'm not sure if this is part of the mythology of AIDS – 'people screwing with fewer people' – but I am sure that gay people are conscious of the dangers. I was surprised at one stage to hear that many people talk very candidly about their fears and how they've reacted; you'd not get that in the straight world and that comforts me.

The past doesn't worry me but the future does. I'm sure I haven't got the virus, but I'm not sure I can avoid it in the future. For instance, I've fallen in love with an American student. He's twenty-one and from San Francisco and he's been out for only two years. We haven't had sex together yet and perhaps we never shall; I'm courting him at the moment. I don't feel I have the right to ask him about past partners in that it may annoy him and compromise his affections for me. If we did start a sexual relationship I could ask him to take an AIDS test. But what if he refused? I feel sure I should still want him. And what if he was antibody positive? I might still decide I want him. Very Tristanesque, I know, death through love, but there we are. Even safe sex is no guarantee against infection. In a way I'm reconciled to dying at an early age. I don't plan for it, but I acknowledge it as a very real possibility. But that was so even before AIDS and my coming out. I'm afraid it's a cynicism about living without much difficulty through an unhappy childhood, the permanent threat of war and self-doubt. If I loved someone enough, I could bear to know it might kill me. In the meantime I worry a little, and play safe. If ever I have sex these days, which isn't often, I practise the safe-sex guidelines. When I had a boyfriend we used, at first, to have anal sex but we gradually stopped that; I didn't enjoy it, and I think we had both begun to realize the dangers. Perhaps I used AIDS as an excuse for saying no. It may sound uncaring, contemptible even, but AIDS has given me the excuse to expect from others the sort of lifestyle I want to lead.

VERNON

I don't feel there is anything to be scared about with regards to AIDS. I feel it is now a calculated risk among the gay community. From what I've observed among the people I know, their promiscuity has not decreased because of the AIDS crisis. I think most young people who, like myself, have only recently come on to the gay scene are fully aware of the safe-sex guidelines. Certainly the position has been made perfectly clear to the members of my youth group in Merseyside at their regular meetings. It can then only be left up to individuals to put them into practice.

I have never personally been tested for HTLV. However, I know somebody who has and who has been diagnosed positive. Although it came as something of a shock to me, I feel the best thing to do is carry on as normal and make sure he knows I'm always there for him. I feel that not alienating him is more important than anything.

GORDON

I'm now twenty and I've been having sex for about five years. I estimate that I've had about two hundred partners. My first experience of a sexually transmitted diseases clinic was one of fear, mostly self-induced, of seeing one of my parents' friends there; however, the doctors and nurses were relatively sympathetic. They were hurried, so had little time, but I doubt very much whether I was treated differently for being gay. My naivety shone through when I was asked whether I had been the active or the passive partner. Thinking that this was a reference to promiscuity I replied, 'Well, quite active'!

My current GP knows I'm gay. With some embarrassment, I must confess, this has less to do with political 'right-on-ism' than with a sense of self-preservation. Because I recently got an HTLVIII positive result I used this to get my GP to write to my college where I was under threat of expulsion, to tell them I had been under great stress and that was the reason I had fallen behind in my work.

His reaction to my being HTLVIII positive can only be described as a perverse sense of glee. After all, as a GP in a grotty little English backwater, it's not often that you get living proof of *Sun* headlines in your surgery! He's very 'understanding' in a

Guardian reader, straight liberal sort of way. He cautioned me about safe sex and transmission of the virus, though I knew far more than he did as since my diagnosis I have become a mini-encyclopaedia on HTLVIII and AIDS.

My only complaints are that the previous GP – at the same college surgery – took a blood test when I originally spoke to him about swollen lymph glands and expressed fears about HTLVIII. What I object to is that he neither discussed with me nor asked my permission to make the test. As it was I probably would have given it anyway. Besides him breaking the law (wow!) I think this is pretty appalling. It was only after I questioned him as to what the blood test was for that he confessed. The nurses in the surgery were completely freaked out by the experience of having to take my blood. Not only was this a poof, but possibly an AIDS-infected one too! So, when they took my blood, they wrapped themselves in virtual space-gear, and all four of them were fluttering around me. Of course they needed to take some precautions, and I know that they are not necessarily going to have the same attitudes towards HTLVIII as a nurse in a London hospital would have, but it was still a bit over the top!

I personally feel 'happier' knowing that I'm HTLVIII positive. It's better than getting worried every time I feel a lump on my neck that I may be. I think I've adjusted fairly well although it's only six months since I found out. It's obviously not something I ever forget about but at the same time I'm not obsessed by it. In fact I don't actually think about it much except when I read a depressing or an uplifting statistic.

I've only told three people: one, a straight man who is a very close friend and who has reacted very supportively; a gay man who is a relatively close friend who I told more because I was completely obsessed with the result for about a week or so after I got it, rather than out of a positive desire to tell him; and a bisexual woman who I know I can trust. There are very few others that I think I will tell. I've not told sexual partners but I have practised safer sex. Whenever I've suggested we use a sheath nearly all of the blokes have been reluctant to do so, even when I point out that I have been promiscuous in London and therefore am likely to be infected.

I regret my GP knowing the result simply because I am going to battle with him to persuade him not to keep it on my medical files which, although supposedly confidential, are nevertheless in the hands of the authorities. I will probably lose.

I actually got my result from an STD clinic in a London hospital. While I understand that they are starved of time and resources in the face of the crisis, I still think they behaved pretty appallingly. They made me feel apologetic when I asked 'too many questions'. Nevertheless their medical treatment has been fine and I certainly haven't been treated as a leper or a freak. I was given my result by a really unsympathetic doctor who hadn't even waited for me to sit down before he said, ' 'Fraid it's positive, old chap', not the best introduction ever!

Knowing I'm HTLVIII positive has calmed my feelings about AIDS, paradoxically perhaps, but I feel that if healthy and quite happy people like me have HTLVIII it can't be too bad to be positive. It has made me quite critical about promiscuity, though not from a moralistic point-of-view, just in the sense that I don't think it leads to satisfaction, and it has made me appreciate what I've got in my life, and how fragile and tenuous everything is.

DAVID

On holiday once I contracted urethral gonorrhoea and attended the clinic on my return. I was duly treated with antibiotics and the condition cleared very quickly; I did, however, get a touch of diarrhoea because of the antibacterial. On attending for a check that things had cleared the doctor asked if I was OK. 'Fine,' I said, 'but it might be useful if you could tell people that the treatment might give diarrhoea.' I said this as, at the time, the great AIDS hysteria was in full flood. Any gay person with diarrhoea may have jumped to the totally wrong conclusion. I explained this to the doctor and she seemed to agree. At this point the nurse attending joined in the conversation, 'Well I wish you would tell your friends, they all think they've got it!' I was stunned to silence by the outburst. It wasn't until later that I realized that if the nurse's attitude was reflected to all gay patients they would have a poor service from that clinic.

Another annoying incident was when the HTLVIII antibody test became available, one of the registrars got on her high horse about it. She spluttered her rage at 'the irresponsible people who didn't want to take the test because the result could interfere with their sex lives'. Unfortunately I was unable to reason with her and change her dogmatic opinion.

AIDS has had an effect on me. When the media campaign started here in the UK about April 1985, I absorbed many of the opinions and became scared to be with a lot of gay people, especially at a disco where I began to find the 'meat market' attitude frightening. It was as if lots of these people were 'carriers of death' and if I had anything to do with them I could get it and die. I was particularly afraid of the promiscuous people that I saw regularly in the disco. It was a very negative period for me as I had just finished a relationship and was looking for somebody to go out with. I was also in need of sexual release particularly as I don't find jerking-off very satisfactory. All of these conflicting attitudes gave me a very poor outlook on life.

Now my attitude is quite different. I know that AIDS is simply another disease with known routes of transmission. Now I know, no matter how many partners you have, as long as you follow safe sex you will be OK. I have been going out with a guy for eight months now and have used safe sex most of the time. Only once has he screwed me without a condom, and he came inside me having misheard me when in mid-stroke I asked him *not* to come inside me. I don't think avoiding anal sex will bother me very much. Some of my friends say anal sex *is* sex for them. They know all about safe sex but find it very difficult to follow. It is a case of 'It'll never happen to me.' Until recently there have been apparently no people with AIDS in the city where I live.

A good friend's ex-lover died recently of a strange 'cancer of the spinal cord'. I have since found strong inferences that he died from AIDS. He was in the regional isolation hospital being treated by one of the AIDS experts. Everyone that knew him insisted that it wasn't AIDS. It's like there's such a stigma attached to AIDS that you can't say someone is suffering from it. Everyone is denying it despite such strong clues. Likewise, I was visiting Edinburgh recently and a guy I knew from years gone by is in hospital seriously ill with cancer. He has lost a lot of weight and is expected to die soon. Everyone suspects AIDS but it's as though there's a tacit agreement to conspire in the denial of it. This annoys me. I'm sad about the chap's illness but feel that gay men in this part of the country should face the facts that AIDS is here now and that the situation is going to get worse unless we all try to stick to safe sex. These two incidents have fixed in my mind that we should be positive about this challenge, not pretend it doesn't exist. I think the only thing worse than people dying of AIDS is the denial of its existence and the subsequent deaths that will happen because of the 'It'll never happen to me' outlook. Maybe it only hits home when everyone has lost a close friend. I hope not.

I haven't been tested for HTLVIII. At first I thought it was a good idea, but now that I know that the test proves nothing, only exposure to the virus, I have changed my mind. Originally I was going to have the test to reassure myself that I hadn't been exposed to it. If the test proved positive I'd be devastated and I know that if it proved negative I'd be falsely reassured that I'm safe. I'm really furious about insurance companies asking about HTLVIII tests. It gives validity to the test – you could be negative tested and then get a positive the next week! – and will be used as a discrimination criterion in jobs despite the lack of risk attached to any other person. On a television programme the other day, medical and ethical quandaries were being posed to a panel of experts. A 'businessman' decided he would sack an employee if it became known that the employee was HTLVIII positive. 'Ah,' said the interviewer, playing devil's advocate, 'but this man is a haemophiliac.' 'Well, then I would have second thoughts about sacking him.' It was obvious that HTLVIII simply gave him a validity for his bigotry against gay men, this despite all the medics on the panel saying the public was not at risk.

It infuriates me, this hierarchy of blame that has developed. Babies are innocent and this is a tragedy. Haemophiliacs are unfortunate if they go antibody positive. Drug addicts are crazed and wish death from the syndrome to satisfy a hunger. Gay men are never innocent and it is implied that they deserve it. I've just heard of another incident. A gay friend of mine in his late forties was due to go into hospital for a repeat operation to one carried out several years ago. He had taken time off work and was waiting in hospital, so he thought, for an operation the next day. The doctor asked to see him privately and enquired whether he had lost weight recently. He had lost weight during the previous year. He was asked if he had had hepatitis or jaundice. By this time he knew where things were leading. He was told that as he was in a high risk group he would have to have the HTLVIII test before they would operate. He was given no counselling before the test and told not to worry as all the tests they had done on other people had proved negative. 'Yes,' said my friend, 'that's all very well. But what if it's positive?' The doctor didn't know what to say. The whole situation is crazy. My friend has been at home nearly two weeks now waiting for the result of the test, and also waiting to see if he will get the operation. It is really appalling that doctors are more influenced by the *Sun* than medical opinion. They are only doing tests on those they know to be 'high risk category patients'. The stupid thing is that a 'happily married man' could be high risk, but unknown. The absurdity, of course, is that even if everyone were tested before an operation there would still be people with the virus who had not, at that point, developed the antibody. It's so crazy and illogical. The medics are behaving as badly, or worse, than the media hacks. They are using pseudo-science to discriminate. One can only presume that if my friend should prove antibody positive then he won't get the operation. OK, so it won't be fatal if he doesn't get this particular operation, but what if it were an anti-body positive person who required emergency surgery? Would the surgeon just let her or him die? The obstetricians seem to be able to cope. They have, already, in my area, delivered babies to several women who are antibody positive. Perhaps it's homophobia, combined with the small risks of surgery, that is reinforcing this discrimination.

AIDS could be used as a new apartheid, except that where I live the largest numbers of HTLVIII cases are among the largely heterosexual drug-taking population. I'm not being complacent about it though and neither are my friends. I've written several letters to government ministers and councillors when they have made derogatory statements. I've even given my name and address on the letters. I think that is a display to myself of how seriously I take the challenge of AIDS. Even a couple of years ago I wouldn't have supplied my name and address but I feel that I have to stand up and be counted. If anyone seriously considered closing gay bars I would certainly be out on the streets demonstrating and I'm sure many, many quiet law-abiding people would be too. We have gone too far to be put back in the closet. Once people have had rights, it's very difficult to take them away again. All of these cries for 'AIDS camps' are extreme views which get media coverage because of that. We shouldn't get paranoid and believe these to be the majority view; but such views should be attacked to prevent them spreading. The greatest danger that I see is complacency. Look what that led to in Germany in the 1930s. I hope that will never happen again: 'AIDS camps' has a ring of familiarity. But if everyone keeps their heads it won't happen. Was it Churchill who once said 'the price of freedom is eternal vigilance'? Even if it wasn't him I couldn't agree more.

These remaining passages have been written since the beginning of 1990

ANDREW

I have lived all my sexual life within the shadow of HIV and AIDS, as I was born in 1973 and did not really become sexually aware until I was fifteen and did not lose my virginity until I was sixteen. HIV has not really affected my practices in that I have always practised safer sex and I would never consider doing anything else. I suppose I was about twelve when HIV first came to my attention, as the great gay plague. I was terribly misinformed about it and assumed that I would die if I ever had sex with another man. That, I suppose, was one of the main reasons for the suppression of my acknowledgement of my true sexual identity.

I don't see the risk in multiple partners as long as safer sex techniques are followed. For a while I had had only two sexual partners, then I asked myself who was I saving myself for and decided to play the field. I feel that I have not compromised my HIV status in any way.

I do voluntary work for an AIDS organization in Glasgow and it gets me very angry when I have heterosexuals who claim they are not the ones at risk. The only person I know to have died was a heterosexual woman, so the attitude of the usually white working-class males that it has nothing to do with them really pisses me off, to the extent that I almost believe that if they become HIV positive then it would be their own fault. I almost do, but I would never wish HIV positive status on anyone.

PAT

The first death of someone I had had sex with was in February 1990, three weeks after we had made love and he had come in my mouth and I had screwed him. PCP and goodnight at thirty-one. I was wild with grief and terror and have been tested and re-tested regularly; so far, so negative! That made me change; no more semen, very protected anal sex; mutual masturbation rules mainly. I'm still not entirely safe as a former lover from England announced he was positive recently. His need for sex involved five or six rentboys a night, drink and drugs, so the result was inevitably what was unthinkable. I was married ten years ago and so multi-partnering was very rare. And yes, I accept that at forty-six I'm not the wildly attractive one that all men are dying to bed; sad that. So, age has played a part, but I don't think I'll risk unprotected sex again.

MICHAEL

I heard the word AIDS echoing around me in the wilderness of my isolation. I was a priggish, precious Victorian girl who vaguely realized that people were dying because of something involving lower limbs. I thought they deserved it these contemptuous people. It was, could be nothing other than, a judgement from God.

Fuck, with a mind like that, who needs tabloids?

I needed something to shock me out of my middle-class complacency. Being gay provided it. When I talk to the figure who would have been me were I not gay, I rather enjoy his embarrassment and disgust, for he is a silly old fool who ignored AIDS health lessons when he was younger because he thought they had no relevance for him, who dismissed it as a gay plague and then caught it while enjoying his heterosexual sex, certified non-injurious to health by God himself.

These lessons were given at my sixth-form college. I was seventeen. I told my mother and stepfather that I considered the lessons irrelevant for 'I will never be in danger of catching it.' I remember very little of the lesson, for the haze of my complacency blocked it out. It was well balanced and not at all judgemental. It stressed the importance of wearing a condom, and we divided sexual acts into groups according to their risk. All I remember of this is that I thought a love bite meant that one person would chomp their way into another's neck – well, people must get hungry when 'doing it'. As you can see sex was as remote an area of knowledge and experience as was cannibalism and probably justifiably analogous.

My only source of information was from the 'impartial' pages of the *Daily Mail*. (Note for readers of the future: this was a publication which claimed to be a newspaper. It wasn't, it simply summarized the prejudices of its readers and defecated them as news. Thus the readership could be content that their beliefs were correct for they had them confirmed every day.)

Thus when this Victorian miss was deflowered a few months later by a twenty-two-year-old ex-soldier, he was scared witless. For, rather like his counterpart who believed she could be made pregnant if a man touched her tummy button, he thought that 'it' could be contracted through mutual masturbation. I telephoned the National AIDS Helpline and was assured I was safe. More importantly I had taken the first step along the thread which led to acceptance of myself. Had it not been for AIDS I would have continued deceiving myself about my sexuality, satisfying it periodically in public lavatories, despising myself more each time I stepped off my secure platform which I called normality but which was, in fact, conformity.

GARETH

The AIDS crisis instantly horrified me but it did not change my behaviour overnight. I was glad I had returned from the States when I did (1978), although I realized I might still have picked up the virus. I continued to visit Manchester and London for promiscuous weekends until one night, as the result of the latest media report, lying in bed I imagined the virus replicating in my body and became convinced that it was only a matter of time before symptoms began to appear. Every time I developed an infection such as bronchitis I thought it might be the onset of the disease and used to mention the possibility to doctors. Depending where I was living at the time they either acted cool (Brighton) or horrified (West Midland suburbs). My present doctor knows I'm gay and just acts slightly embarrassed when the subject comes up.

From early on AIDS affected my ambitions and self-confidence. I no longer wanted to take career risks involving different types of work or a move to another part of the country or abroad. I did not want to go partying or miss a night's sleep. I figured

that anything which put undue pressure on my body's immune
system would be enough to set the disease in motion. I once
went for the HIV test in Brighton, having let a man fuck me
who later said he'd slept with a local guy who'd died of AIDS.
However, when it was time for the result the nurse asked me
whether I really wanted it. I knew he meant 'What difference
would it make?', so I told him to forget it. At that time (1984)
there was little anybody could do and I knew about the risks of
a false sense of confidence from a *negative* result. During the next
few years a number of people I'd known and had sex with at
different times died of AIDS. This was a shocking and depressing
time. Perhaps the only reason I don't still know of friends with
AIDS is that I've been largely off the scene. I don't often have
sex now.

RICHARD

Earlier this year I discovered that I was HIV negative. Having
entered into a monogamous exclusive relationship, the two of us
decided to get tested. This was, in part, because we wanted to
be able to practise 'unsafe' sex and, in part, because it seemed
sensible to know where we stood since neither of us would have
liked to have discovered, perhaps years later, that we had infected
the other. My head tells me that this means I have a reactionary
unreconstructed perspective on homoeroticism, but my cock tells
me otherwise. Fairly early on in any relationship the question of
trust comes up. How can you really trust someone who continues
to insist on condoms some months into a relationship. Is the
relationship as exclusive as you thought it was? This led us, and
leads many people, into having tests too early in a relationship
to be confident that we had been HIV negative throughout the
relationship. Safer sex campaigns have not yet addressed this
issue.

   The impact of AIDS in my life is much as it was when I wrote
my report in 1986. I continue to meet people through my work
with an AIDS charity purely on account of their HIV status. At
the same time friends continue to become infected, to discover
they are infected, to get sick and to die. I do not react in the
way that I used to – the feeling of the waste of such talent and
potential; I think I respond more to the individual than the issue
now.

I almost take the fact of AIDS, among gay men in particular, for granted. Both my partner and I were surprised to be HIV negative and felt that we 'deserved' to be positive since we had done just about everything just about as often as others who we knew were positive. I know that this is self-victimization but James Thompson reports similar feelings among the survivors of disasters.

The friends and friends of friends that I have lost to AIDS are about to reach three figures. I attend memorial services as long as they are not religious. Organized religion has killed far more gays than AIDS has.

I have not seen much evidence of a change in lifestyles, to be honest. People have been frightened off some forms of sex, but they are the people who were frightened off by hepatitis. On the scene I see that what went on still goes on and the values of the gay scene in London are those of promiscuity and licence. I know a lot of people who are still in the fast lane and their life of high risk sex and drugs and alcohol has not changed at all. They may use condoms . . . sometimes. I know what happens on Hampstead Heath and other cruising areas and in beds all over London and I can assure you that condoms are not that much in evidence.

The *Sun* still writes of 'the myth of heterosexual AIDS'. When I saw recently that the figures on HIV rates are now higher for straights than for gays, then I am ashamed to say that I did feel glad. But they continue to see it as a gay plague and, frankly, I do not think that movies like *Longtime Companion* or novels like *Eighty-Sixed* or Armistead Maupin's books do anything to stop this. If my attitude has changed at all then I think it is from cynicism to resignation.

KEVIN

There it was one day, all of a sudden, that purplish lump. I didn't run to the clinic for a diagnosis but when I finally called in and KS was confirmed I felt disorientated; later I cried. But then I took stock. KS is only an AIDS indicator, not life-threatening in itself. So far I've had only a string of little illnesses. My AIDS diagnosis has actually come as a kind of relief. I'm no longer dreading its arrival. It's here and I'm dealing with it one day at a time. I plan, at the very least, to see in the new millennium. . . .

8

Pride

A special area of any mass-observation programme is the 'day-diary', when volunteers are invited to record everything they can of their activities on a given day. Each group of NL&GS observers is asked for a day-diary for a particular last Saturday in June, Britain's official day for celebrating Lesbian and Gay Pride, whether or not the day's activities involve anything to do with Pride, or even whether or not her or his sexuality has an explicit bearing on the events of the day.

IAN

During the early hours of 27 June 1987 I was at the Market Tavern, dancing, drinking and socializing. This is one of my favourite bars and I go often enough to know a fair amount of people there. It was quite crowded, no doubt more so than usual because of an influx of visitors to London for the Pride march. It was on a Gay Pride weekend about two or three years ago that I was first taken there. As arranged, I met a friend there who later drove me home and came in for a couple of hours, leaving at around 3 am after we had enjoyed a heavy sex scene together. I was worried about the amount of noise we were making as I knew the neighbours would be able to hear. At 6.55 am the alarm clock in the flat above went off, which may well have been her revenge.

Shortly after this rude awakening I had sex with Jack my lover, then brought him orange juice and tea in bed. His hay fever was particularly bad that morning and I tried to be as sympathetic as possible. A friend telephoned and we arranged to meet at a pub in Poland Street prior to going on the march. Loud music was coming from the flat above and we discussed our problems with our neighbours who were also in the process of re-fencing their garden and generally causing us a lot of inconvenience. Before catching the underground Jack went to the chemists for something to alleviate his hay fever, while I went to join the long queue for the cash dispenser outside the bank. One of the topics of conversation on the tube was Jack's health. He was complaining of sweating much more than he used to. His fear was that he might be HIV positive and we discussed whether he would go for a test to find out. Since we had not discussed this in depth before, and there was not time to go into all its aspects, I suggested we leave the topic until one of the regular evening 'meetings' we have when we talk over everything on our minds. The topic of AIDS has, of course, come up before in our conversation but never so immediately and definitely as this.

It was humid and overcast and I wondered if the march would ever be held in ideal weather conditions again. It was my fourth march and Jack's first. At the pub which was so full people were crowding on to the pavement outside, I met a number of friends and bought a round of drinks for about eight people, consisting almost entirely of orange juices and soda, a reflection, no doubt, of the over-indulgence of the night before. I was introduced to someone and chatted to him at length. Then we set out to walk to Speakers' Corner for the beginning of the march. As usual it was impressive to see so many different groups there, many with banners, and such a wide variety of people. As we marched I met and talked to a number of old friends, also a number of strangers. It was, as ever, interesting to observe the reactions of the onlookers. I felt most impressed and uplifted when we crossed the river and the procession doubled back on itself and under the bridge, making it possible to see just how long it was.

Arriving at Jubilee Gardens on the South Bank I met a friend who I have known for a few months and flirted with, but who has never taken anything further before. He told me about his private life, more than I had heard before, and said that he would welcome a therapeutic S/M bonk that evening to relieve some of his tension. I gave him instructions as to when and how to turn up later, and we parted. I came home by tube which seemed to be full of gay people. I chatted to a group of three gay men I had not met before, also to a man on his own who I thought was rather weird and who alarmed me by following me home even though I had said goodbye to him. Jack was home and we chatted and compared notes on the march since we had separated and walked with different groups. We washed and changed and Jack went out again to see a friend in north London where he was to stay the night.

About 10.30 the doorbell rang and I was unsure whether this was the friend I expected, as I had instructed him to ring from a call-box en route, or someone else. Fortunately – since I was dressed in my leather gear which might have been difficult to explain had it been a neighbour or a straight friend – it was him. I had a good idea what he wanted and gave him a suitably rough time, blindfolding and handcuffing him as a start. We played for an hour and a half. Then, shortly after midnight we went to bed together and chatted about the day and lots of other things.

RICHARD

27 June 1987 . . . Brunch on two cheese sarnies and a very large gin and tonic and listen to Rachmaninov's second piano concerto while I agonize over what to wear, one of my few concessions to gay stereotypy. I shall have to include the scarf Margaret (now suffering in a camp for American kids – serve her right for deserting me!) made for me last autumn. It's made of blue silky material embroidered with large pink triangles. Not exactly work-aday wear, even for someone as flamboyant as myself, but I did solemnly swear that I'd wear it on the march and Margaret will demand photographs to prove it, though it's not exactly scarf weather. The diamante hat-pin holds it in place around my waist quite nicely. Otherwise I settle for black (with yellow braces) the colour I always wear when I can't make up my mind.

The second question of the day is which banner to march under. I have a commitment to a lesbian and gay teachers group, to my local gay and lesbian group, to a gay theatre group and to the Terrence Higgins Trust. Oh, and I almost forgot, there'll be a banner for the Hall-Carpenter Archives like last year too.

I am one of those insufferables who bully the rest of you into attending Gay Pride Day. At the Hippo, the Fallen Angel and the Gay Centre I have concluded every parting with 'see you on the march, Saturday'. That dates me this year; I notice it's being marketed as a 'parade'. I much prefer the more militant 'march'; but then, as I've said before, I sometimes feel I'm the only person who still believes in Gay Liberation.

Nice to be able to join in with singing 'Glad to be Gay' on the Central Line. I think we are fewer than last year though it's hard to tell. THT have a coachful so I join the teachers' group. I mingle for a while chatting to old friends, complimenting Mike on his new book, Tommy on his new hairstyle and being introduced to Glen's new lover. The march was enjoyable. Someone should record the chants: 'Two, four, six, eight! Is your husband really straight?' 'Three, five, seven, nine! Don't worry, neither's mine!' and a new one, 'Give us an "O"; give us another "O"; give us another "O"; what have you got? "OOOH!" ' in both a standard and an orgasmic version. . . . Interested to see a banner from my home town, there wasn't one in my day. . . . Fritz leaves us to plant a kiss on the cheek of a little old lady in Piccadilly. . . . 'Oh, look out for the Fortnum's queens!' . . . singing 'When the gays go marching in' . . . chants of 'Burn it down' outside the South African embassy . . . interesting interpretations of 'Woman in Mind' and 'Me and My Girl' from the sisters as we pass the theatres where they're on. . . .

LARRY

27 June 1987 . . . I feel lazy and indecisive. I know I'm not going to get very much done today. I need to get the measure of this. If I just laze around I'll get to the end of the day feeling hellish; if I attempt too much I'll fail to get it done and still feel hellish. Also I am still seething about what happened yesterday. About three months ago a colleague of mine was suspended following allegations which concerned sexual activity with a young person. This had subsequently been subject to a police investigation and the police had dropped the matter. Yesterday he was asked in for a disciplinary hearing which I attended as shop steward. What happened was that, although they didn't attempt to pursue the original allegations, they nevertheless issued a warning on the basis that his conduct was out of keeping with his role as an employee. The implication appears to be that he or I or anybody can do things in his personal life which are perfectly legal, which break no rules of any sort, which give rise to no complaints of any substance and as a result of which nobody or nothing can be shown to be harmed, and yet you might be sacked for it. . . .

3.45 pm. I feel listless. I want some company. I decide to go into town to a gay bar. Am I going to cruise? I'm not sure; I'll see when I get there. What, therefore, to wear? I decide on my leather jacket, and I take a cockstrap in my pocket and leave it at that. Too strong a signal might give the impression that I have more energy than is, in fact, the case. Buy some cigarettes and chocolate. Catch bus. Once we get into town the buses are snarled up. This is usual on Saturdays ever since deregulation so I get off and walk the last few hundred yards. I count twenty-eight buses heading, or rather not heading, east, one behind the other. There's no other traffic. Just buses. Jesus Christ.

4.10 pm. I arrive in the bar and find a pleasant corner. Order drink. See a man who looks interesting. He leaves instantly. Drink arrives. Various other men look interesting and attractive. What am I going to do? The options are: (a) I stay here where there's nobody I particularly know, or (b) I go to the nearby bookshop where I know the staff, or (c) I go and visit Caroline. I don't make the decision and so, by default, I just stay. A man comes in and makes small talk, but no particular conversation ensues and then his friend arrives and after a few minutes they leave.

A leather-jacketed young man arrives and sits on the stool next to mine. I see from his jacket that it has started to rain. We chat for a few minutes but conversation stops. After a while he pulls out the Motorcycle Social Club's newsletter and I ask him if he's a member; he's not but he's enquiring about joining. We talk about our shared diffidence about leather. For him it's mainly about particular activities; for me it's not the activities which bother me but the masonic aspect of it all. Male secret societies are pretty dubious, aren't they?

6.00 pm. He says he's about to go home and would I like to go too. I'm a little surprised as I have indicated that I'm a confirmed 'bottom man' and while he hasn't said anything very clearly my impression was that he is too. So I hesitate, then agree and apologize for hesitating. We leave. On the way up the road we exchange names. Get a taxi. He tells me he's unemployed. He had used to work in a gay disco in town but he'd been sacked. It strikes me it's easy to get sacked from there and he agreed. He said he doesn't get out much as the giro doesn't go far. He had just received his housing benefit cheque but it was postdated and the post office wouldn't cash it. This had wrecked his day.

Small talk, coffee, beer, sex. For two bottom men we do quite well. As usual, as soon as I've had an orgasm I want to cuddle and sleep which we do (and I think I'll make a leatherman!). We wake up around 8.30. The predictable hiatus. I know I'm supposed to leave before his sister and her boyfriend get in from work but does he want me to leave right now? He rings a Chinese carry-out and orders food for one and this seems to clear the matter up, so I wash and dress, smoke a cigarette and make my goodbyes.

I feel stiff and sleepy and decide to walk despite the rain. I realize how hungry I am. I walk through a park which is sometimes cruisy but nobody's about. Once through I decide to look for something to eat. I decide on a pancake roll but seem to find every form of food except Chinese. Get the pancake roll. There's a bus stop right outside and there's a bus coming. Good. But it doesn't stop at this particular stop. I feel foolish and try to make it appear that I didn't want to catch it and start to walk. After about three hundred yards I wait at a bus stop. To get home I will need to change buses near the pub where I was earlier. So I decide to go in for a pint. The usual crowd is there so I talk to them. Billy, the doorman comes by, talks to me and feels my bum. I used to have an amazing crush on him and he would flirt with me and wind me up. Then for months he didn't speak to me at all. Now I'm over the crush I can just enjoy the flirt. More small talk. Home by eleven. Frankenstein film. Sleep.

STEPHEN

I first met Jan at a Safe Sex party in Amsterdam in February and we began an extensive correspondence soon after, interrupted only by my visiting him over Easter and his spending ten days with me shortly afterwards. I thought it would be interesting to spend Gay Pride day in Holland.

The march itself didn't take place in Amsterdam; it hasn't been there for well over ten years. Instead, they have it in provincial towns: last year it was Utrecht, the year before in Gröningen and next year it will be in Delft. This year it was in Enschede, a university town in the east, not far from the German border, and scarcely central for travel. So we left Amsterdam at 9 am on the morning of 27 June in a coach booked by COC. We'd been at the COC disco only seven hours before so we were both very tired. And I was feeling depressed. Our relationship was going through its first bad patch, though nothing major. It was just that the journey of discovery up to then had been a beautiful thing. Now I had begun to feel a few bad things, and that's what I thought about on the journey to Enschede, wondering if our relationship would survive these first doubts – and reflecting on how little time Jan and I had actually spent together in the week I had been with him. He had much work to do and dinners were usually spent with friends – his friends – most of whom I think I would find very shallow even if I understood Dutch. I felt a little annoyed, but I understood what was happening and why I was feeling as I did; that made it somewhat easier. But still I wondered if I loved Jan; I decided I did, though yes, things would be easier if I didn't. All these thoughts opened up thoughts about previous relationships and how such an emotional attachment had led to pain and suffering when it seemed we were drifting apart, and how I had been even ill with worry at the time.

And then we sat together on the coach and put our arms around each other. My cares vanished in a moment and did not reappear that day, surfacing later in the week, but again to be dissipated by his love and affection, and by our talking over our problems.

Enschede itself is a small town, two hours from Amsterdam, and we arrived just before noon, two hours before the march was planned to start. Everyone seemed to be assembling at an information fair near the centre. We had a look round, buying a few souvenirs and a copy of Rita May Brown's *Rubyfruit Jungle*. Jan showed me the S/M group stall, the parents' support group and the gay soldiers' group! I explained how homosexuality is still an offence for the military in England. How can two so completely different approaches be reconciled?

This, like all Pride events, was a social occasion as much as a political statement. Jan met friends from distant times and places, and an ex-boyfriend from Gröningen. Even I met someone I knew – the boy I met on my very first stay in Amsterdam. I also met an ex of mine from England; I would have preferred not to have met him. Jan, his ex and I drank coffee by the market square till the church bells summoned us to march.

The march itself fell below my expectations. It was very small – only about three thousand – and not quite the extravagant or extrovert affair I had imagined. Perhaps here they have less to be radical about, though Enschede itself hardly offers a picture of untramelled deviancy. That, of course, is why it was chosen. The

Dutch believe that having a Pride march in Amsterdam has virtually no impact. Everyone in Amsterdam knows about lesbians and gays and, to some degree, tolerates them. The real battle is to be fought in the provinces, the rural areas and the Catholic south. So the venue is rotated each year. The English may care to consider this approach. Perhaps a Pride march in Rugby would do more good for lesbians and gays than the carnival affair in London.

Of course, there was the kissing and the hugging. But then here it goes on all the time. In England it is much more a symbol of defiance. Jan and I kissed for the benefit of the crowd, and the beautiful young men along the roads. They seemed amused more than anything else. Perhaps its effect would be felt much later. Then suddenly the march came to its end, back at the Vogelpark. And, again, the relatively small scale of the thing struck me: not so many stalls as at Jubilee Gardens or Kennington, only about half a dozen. Not even a beer tent, can you imagine? Boring speeches from city officials; pop music; a few raindrops to remind me of last year; and thoughts about the internationalism of sexuality and the very different responses of different countries and of the communities within these countries. The different battles yet to win and the differing motivations of those fighting. Holland had gained so much – had it undermined its radicalism? England had gained so little – formally at least – and yet the movement could still hardly be thought of as radical. Thoughts of moving to Holland; depressed at the state of the gay struggle in England. . . .

MATTHEW

One thing I have got very clear over these three weeks is how much I am missing Ralph. We met only a couple of months ago but already this is perhaps the most serious relationship I have ever entered. During the earlier week I made a commitment to be present in Ralph's life and to commit myself to a relationship with him. I have phoned him twice to tell him some of this. Now I have changed the day of my departure and booked an earlier flight in order to be with him. If I am to be committed to him, the place it starts is here, now. It is no sacrifice to be going home. I am excited that at eight o'clock on Monday morning I shall walk off the plane at Prestwick and he will be there to meet me. This thought returns to me throughout the whole day.

Down on the waterfront near Fisherman's Wharf I visit one of the places I have found the most exciting in San Francisco – Pier 39 – crowded with shops that are different. I want to buy a special sweatshirt for which I have a graphic design to be airsprayed onto the front and the back by the artist working in the back of the shop. The shirt reflects all the things I have gained from my transatlantic trip. The artist is intrigued and we spend time talking about what I have been doing. He gets a sense of the excitement and conveys this to his artwork on the shirt; those standing and watching him wonder what it is all about.

Rather than take a cable-car, I decide to walk back across the city. This city certainly has a lot of hills, but it is clean and friendly. Having dropped off my shopping I wander out again to find a small cafe for a drink.

In some ways it is ironic that I am returning tomorrow. Sunday 28 June is the day of San Francisco's gay parade, perhaps the biggest in the world. I read somewhere that it has taken thirty people all last year to prepare for it and that thousands and thousands of people will be out in the streets just to watch it. Later on I pick up a copy of the *Bay Area Reporter* which is full of goodwill messages from city officials, politicians and others. There are to be speeches, rallies, concerts, open-air events and a host of other attractions right across the city. I have chosen to miss all this just to be with Ralph.

As evening falls I wander around the waterfront before strolling back through the streets, past landmarks I have visited earlier in the trip. From a sense of time-fulfilling I have created a whole lot of new experiences that I might otherwise have missed. I would like to eat Mexican tonight and choose a small diner nearly opposite the hotel. The food is OK though not wonderful and I return to the hotel to finish packing, showering and preparing for an early morning departure. Tomorrow I shall be on my way to Ralph.

PHILIP

30 June 1990. A very far from typical day in that I have travelled up to London from the north west the previous day to witness, for the first time, a Gay Pride carnival. On my arrival I had

immediately made for the home of a Gay and Lesbian Humanists Association member to whose pre-Pride party I had been invited. I left fairly early and, tired after a day's travelling, went to bed early. I was staying at an ex-servicemen's club I have belonged to for some years. Unfortunately my room was right on the main road and, despite double-glazing, the deep thunder of the all-night traffic had me sleeping fitfully most of the night. I woke woozily at about 5.30. It was close, the windows being tight shut, and the early morning sun bright in the room.

When I joined the club in the early 1960s it was very rare to see a woman there at all. Then slowly one noticed an increase in married couples. Now there are lots of women and elderly men in very casual wear: open-necked shirts, cotton slacks and even pumps. But still many most attractive white thatched and grey-haired stalwarts. I wondered how many of these fine fellows were aware of the sexual opportunities available. Perhaps more than one would think. At any rate there has been a sexual undercurrent as long as I have been a member; not quite so much now as when I first joined when it was possible to have shared accommodation. I always used to take a sharing room as not only was it cheaper – seven shillings and sixpence a night when I joined – but nine times out of ten one's fellow room occupant was also interested in fun. Now these sharing rooms are used by the married couples. It seems certain that the management knew what was going on. The toilets – several to each floor – were also incredible. These have now been remodelled in different ways, making cruising unsuitable. However, the television lounges are still much used, the back rows being the scene of much groping and later, when less crowded, wanking and even trouser-dropping! Over the years I have met many fine men there: an airline pilot from New Zealand, a genuine Kentucky colonel whom I conducted round the Wellington museum at Apsley House and, as all the allies and their forces are admissible for membership, a Danish author.

After a morning spent at the Portobello Road street market, I took the train to Kennington and arrived at the park about two o'clock. I soon located the GALHA stall and a friend of mine who was helping there joined me and we walked around the still quite quiet grounds. We bought a large carton of fresh orange juice and a creamy strawberry gateau. I snapped a photo from time to time of the passing show, a few of the stalls. Shortly afterwards we saw the first people from the march entering and I got some shots of the marchers and their banners; alas many of the banners had been ripped by the winds and were either furled or in unreadable tatters. After taking several shots, I photographed several of the pretty policemen who seemed to have been hand-picked for the job. I forgot to time the march but I heard later that it was over an hour from the first arrivals to the last. The atmosphere was heady and the grounds jam-packed with bodies, some beauties.

I had a meal at the club and rested and read in the lounge. I then spotted an old face I remembered from earlier visits. I must, regretfully, call him an old queen, and I'm sure he would agree. But he was a useful source of information as to what had been happening at the club during all those years I had not been there. He was not a resident but lived locally and used the club as a useful social centre, as indeed it is for many Londoners; a gentle, unmalicious soul.

I went across the road to Speakers' Corner but it was windy and cold, so I returned to the club and went to bed. But despite my tiredness it was some time before sleep came, my head being so full of the excitement of the day's activities.

LUKE

After several days camping in hot sunny weather on beautiful, breathtaking beaches near Land's End I feel like giving something back to the natural world – the great goddess spirit – so what better way to spend a wild, changeable, though dryish morning?

I drive to the beach down very narrow lanes and get busy filling sacks with the plastic flotsam and the rope-ends and so forth strewn disfiguringly all over the beach. Clouds roll over, the sun coming and going, an occasional shower. I have no top on, jeans, wellingtons, no underwear. The waves roar up and suck back; I feel in process with my surroundings, quite hot but satisfied with eight bags full and most of the beach cleared, looking as beautiful as it has for many a millennium, long before we had thought of ourselves.

I get ready to leave as a couple arrives in an expensive car. They get out and watch at the edge of the cliff above the beach and don't venture down. I'm rather judgemental and disparaging in my mind, thinking they've sold themselves for their expensive perks!

I set off along remote and rarely used lanes with glimpses of incredibly wild rocky coast. I'm headed for a pottery friends have told me about – ceramics, a great love of mine; it moves me in the guts. I talk with the potters, women and men, and slowly choose some things. I've not bought pottery in years and I have a binge. Then I drive to a 'green' fair, arriving too late to see my friends' dance performance, but enjoy two men playing sitars.

Back to my friends' place, late afternoon; fall asleep for a couple of hours, luxurious feeling. Turn and roll, and enjoy the feeling of my waking, and my sensory body. . . .

CHARLES

Saturday 29 June 1991. Impruneta Firenze, Italia.

8.00 am. Woke up after spending my first night at the home of a gay friend in this enchanting region of Italy. As I gazed around the bedroom and saw the early morning sun blazing through the shutters and smelt the scent of mimosa bushes drifting in on a gentle breeze, I had to pinch myself while I stretched my arms and legs in order to accept the fact that I was actually on holiday and away from the rain and mist of my home town miles away in northern England. I then thought about the evening before when I had flown in and was met by my dear old friend and his beautiful live-in lover, how we had greeted each other with a hug and a kiss that told us both that our long absence apart had not altered our mutual feelings for each other. I then thought of what I would have been doing back at home in the UK, waking up in a hotel room in London and looking forward to taking part in Gay Pride Day and meeting Kerry and Ken.

8.20 am. My host enters the room bearing a pot of coffee which is most welcome, made from coffee beans and freshly ground. After exchanging greetings in Italian we kissed, quite customary in this country between males but more natural, in our case, being gay.

Ten minutes later I got up out of my bed and putting on my robe opened the shutters and stepped out on to the balcony outside and gazed at the panoramic view of the village below. A number of locals were already going about their daily tasks. This being primarily a farming community I spotted a drover with his goats wending his way toward the fields and a flat cart pulled by a tired looking horse. . . .

At 10.30 we set out to visit Florence City where we intended spending the best part of the day. We lunched at a small *ristorante* run by a family who were noted for their home-made pasta dishes. I had a minestrone type of soup followed by tagliatelle smothered in a mixture of minced meat and tomato sauce; a glass or two of vino rosso with the main dish and then the house special. It has always fascinated me to think of the vast range of flavours, colour and body that emerge from the grape.

In the early afternoon we sat on a bench under the trees on the avenue and watched the scores of people walking by, especially noting the many beautiful young men passing, each of whom elicited the usual sigh from me; how I adore the male form. Feeling contented after a more than satisfying lunch I could easily have sought the company of one of a number of those dark-eyed, sallow-skinned, tight-jeaned males and made love. I find the Italians so warm and friendly, unrushed or ruffled by the tempo of modern life, ever ready to talk with a foreigner and be openly demonstrative too by showing their affections, holding hands and kissing in public without the fear of adverse comments or odd looks that we have to suffer in England.

After visiting many art galleries in this art centre city and calling into several main stores we returned to my friend's home by local bus and enjoyed listening to the gossip of the locals on the journey. After dinner we all sat and listened to records, operatic arias and then some Beethoven especially for me. I watched the exchange of glances between my friends. It gave me a wonderful feeling of what togetherness really means when two men are truly, deeply in love with each other. It also made me just a teeny bit sad that I would have to return to England the next day and the loneliness of my own tiny bungalow.

We talked about the current gay scene in both England and Italy and I realized that, although they do not have the proliferation of gay and lesbian advisory and consultative organizations in Italy that we have in England, this was due to the more open, liberated, accepting attitude of the Italian population generally towards gay men and women, this despite the fact that Italy is a predominantly very religious country where strict observance of the Catholic code of conduct should, in fact, preclude homosexual practices. It was evident that lesbians and gay men in Italy were not exposed to the repressive laws we have had imposed upon us in England. Sex magazines, hard-core pornography even, are openly on sale in all bookshops and corner newspaper kiosks. I remember having great difficulty in persuading my local newsagent to order me *Gay Times*. When I went to collect the first issue he handed it to me actually wrapped in paper as if it was something illegal!

The day came to an end. A memorable day, not just because of the way I had spent it, here with my friends in Italy, but also because I was never far away from the purpose of what this day means to all gay men and women wherever they were, as we who are proud brothers and sisters of the gay fraternity have a bond of mutual understanding that will outlast the relationships formed within the heterosexual world.

RAYMOND

Saturday 27 June 1992. The day started not at home but at a friend's (Chuck's) house in East London. I came down to London the previous evening to meet with friends from a national (and occasionally international) computer-based discussion group for gays, lesbians and bisexuals. Chuck, who manages and organizes the group, roused me at about 9 am, though I had been awake thinking about my boyfriend who was at a wedding in France that day and couldn't come to Pride. Last year was my first Pride celebration and we had spent a wonderful day together walking arm-in-arm – I didn't know what I would get up to today!

At around 9.30 am two more friends, Ed and Billy, arrived after a night at Madame Jo Jo's in Soho and sleeping at another house. I hadn't seen Ed since a trip to Oxford in June 1991 to watch the gorgeous lycra-clad men rowing in the college bumps and it was wonderful to see him again. At that time I had been out six months and had found him intimidating and too openly sexual, but after a year of being out my views had changed and now I found him friendly, fun, raunchy and very easy to get on with. During the preparations to leave he persuaded me to have my hair tinted flamingo pink with hair dye, so I sat bare-chested in the back garden on a kitchen chair while he applied the dye, avoiding my forehead as best he could. I have a quiff at the front and a very short hair cut, which my boyfriend cut (as an amateur) before he left for France. Pink was very appropriate for the day so all three of us were treated. Billy had a pink low-rise Mohican which turned out purple on his black and silver combination hair. I had a pink quiff which looked salmon pink on my mildly ginger and brown hair and Ed attempted a pink moustache with no success: the wash-out-able dye wouldn't take to it. After about twenty minutes we could wash the treatment off to reveal the splendour of the pink. Fashion is a big thing for queers, or for some of us. Chuck had a T-shirt specially delivered that morning with the logo of his organization together with the message 'Have You Cuddled Your Faggot Today?' Billy wore a green shirt, T-shirt and leather jacket with Doc Marten's boots. He was probably, given the sunny and muggy weather, the worst fashion victim. Ed wore a blue 'Freddy the Dolphin' T-shirt and very trendy sunglasses and shorts. I wore a home-made T-shirt with a Tom of Finland design of two men kissing, taken from a phoneline ad in *Gay Times*, superimposed over a pink triangle, a pair of green Marks and Spencer's shorts and a blue shirt to stop my skin from burning. Unfortunately my T-shirt was 100 per cent polyester which wasn't a good choice in the heat. I hadn't been sure whether to wear a 'Pop Against Homophobia' T-shirt also showing two men kissing (nice theme!) but decided to suffer the polyester for the sake of individuality!

After a quick breakfast we grabbed our home-made banner and left the house to catch a bus to the march. My boyfriend and I made the banner last year but it had been such hard work that no permanent logo had been attached. A friend had helped me till 2 am to sew on the logo. It was hard work and we had to miss *The Golden Girls* and a good part of the first programme in the *OUT* series on Channel Four *and* Julian Clary's *Sticky Moments*, so we had suffered to make the 5ft × 6ft banner!

On our way we noticed a few lesbians and gay-looking men, some carrying banners and some just dressed in a very gay manner. We very quickly got a bus to the city centre. As we approached the Embankment the noise level from the Outrage whistles increased as did the number of queers. Soon we had to push our way through the crowds towards the Embankment Underground Station. Everybody we passed was buzzing with excitement and chatting, looking around at others trying perhaps to *spot the straight*.

We erected our flag on the gate in the gardens and waited for others to find us, the only sensible thing to do with the huge number of people. We noticed a couple of gorgeous transvestites, both very thin, black, with long hair and one with knee-length rubber boots. They were outrageous! I went in search of a whistle. I had forgotten the one I had last year, the one with the crappy pea. I didn't find one in the huge crush of people. I was only gone a few minutes but by the time I got back to the banner more of our group had arrived and everything had become more confusing. Reg, an outrageous guy with a nipple clamp and a chain disappearing into the flies of his denims from the side pocket. Joseph, a friend from home who I had travelled down with the day before. Although he had been out as a gay man for six years it was his first Pride march. Phil, also from home, was there with mangled cheese sandwiches and Trevor a London-based programmer who had shaved off his beard the night before. In addition George arrived from West Yorkshire. He'd only been out a few months and it was his first Pride march. He was very excited and enthusiastic about it. He had a whistle but was slightly too self-conscious at that stage to use it with gusto. Christopher, our Euro-cuteling, accompanied George after meeting him the evening before at Madame Jo Jo's.

Without much sense of direction the group of about twelve of us went through the tube station entrance. Whistles from other queers were being blown furiously. The crush was wonderful. A station guard looking fed up was standing in the doorway. We pushed our way down the parade trying to get to a quiet patch, all following the banner which Ed and I held up as high as we could. At the beginning of the march there was a huge number of assorted banners, though none of the *Socialist Worker* placards which were so obvious at last year's parade. Joseph rushed off and bought us both a whistle. In what may become a tradition the pea in my whistle was crappy and the noise was either intermittent and loud or gentle and un-outraged. Still half the fun was blowing it so perhaps in future I'll take a whistle without a pea and save my ears!

Instead of joining the parade at the end we slotted in close to the beginning which saved us pushing down the whole length of the march. Almost immediately the march started, Ed and I still holding the banner. For a while nobody talked to me or marched beside me and I felt a bit peeved at being stuck at the end of the banner, missing sharing all the march experiences with my boyfriend. Very shortly afterwards, however, I met some friends. We had a long cuddle and chat to get up-to-date with news and gossip. Whenever a bus, particularly a London Tour bus, passed the parade everybody blew their whistles and waved. Disappointingly, the streets weren't thronged with onlookers. I think some of the straights had fled from the area. Radio 4 had apparently announced that morning that there would be delays in London due to a march, but didn't say what the marchers were there for!

We were among the first people to reach Hyde Park, though there were large crowds there. As we entered the gates into the park I noticed a chap with a beard from NL&GS who was giving out information. Collapsing in the shade of a tree, leaving the banner resting against the trunk we had a good rest. Reg, Ed and another guy all lay on each other, three layers thick; the rest of us flaked out. All the time more marchers were continually arriving, including about a dozen men dressed only in loose-fitting Calvin Klein underwear, dance/marching in formation to huge cheers and whistling. Joseph, Trevor and myself spent a few minutes checking out the men in the march, appreciating the underwear-clad dancers and a few other individuals.

Transport from Hyde Park to the festival at Brockwell Park was a big problem, especially for people not from London. The BR mainline tracks were closed for repair and the Pride organizers had organized a small fleet of coaches. We decided to take the tube as it occurred to us that the roads to Brockwell Park might be jammed because the traffic near Victoria was at a standstill. The platform was crowded with gays and lesbians and a few straights. People were blowing whistles and chatting. The noise was LOUD. I assumed the people looking annoyed or fed up and holding their ears weren't involved in the march. The first train to arrive terminated there. When it arrived loads of whistle-blowing marchers alighted, adding to the crowds on the platform at what I thought was an increasingly dangerous-looking level. Eventually an announcement came over the tannoy, 'Could you please stop blowing your whistles, you are deafening my staff', which meant, of course, whistles were blown all the louder – though, of course, my pea was giving me trouble again. The announcer again tried to get a message over the noise of the crowds, 'Because of you people and your march you have brought the Underground to a standstill. The next train will not be taking any passengers. Don't get on the next train!' More whistle blowing. The train stopped. A few people managed to crowd on. The train was full of queers and so nobody on or off the platform minded. . . .

The train had to wait a minute in the tunnel before Brixton to allow the congestion in the station to subside. The guard had announced this and told us to expect things to get sweaty – he wasn't wrong. My polyester T-shirt had melded with my skin. When the train got moving again the breeze was wonderful. . . .

There were swarms of people in the park. We headed towards the mud-wrestling and health tents but found ourselves at the section marked 'Sisters of Perpetual Indulgence' on the map. When we arrived one of us asked them to explain a little about what they do. There were about six sisters. The one we spoke to was from New York, though most of them in the park were from the UK. We had arrived at the beginning of an inauguration of four new sisters into the London Order. It was also announced that the London Order was being given autonomy from the New York one. Unfortunately the crowd watching the ceremony wasn't very large – twelve people at that point – so the cheer was a bit lukewarm. The Mother Superior, or Head Sister, waved some incense and holy water substitute at us, telling us about the significance of the ceremony and the potential toxicity of the water which was sprinkled from the kind of bottle used by men to pee into in hospital beds. It seemed to be taking a long time to get nowhere and I left. . . .

My Pride day finished in the same friend's house where it had begun, chatting over a coffee and preparing for bed in a much shorter time than usual. I left the (uncomfortable) sofa-beds for Ed and Billy, opening them out and pushing them together so they wouldn't have to do it quietly when they got back from the London Apprentice at 2 or 4 am. The last thing I did before sleeping was to check a flan recipe for a barbecue the next day, committing the pastry ingredients to memory from one of Chuck's old *Good Housekeeping* books. . . .

Index of authors

The details given in brackets indicate the year and place of each writer's birth and his occupation and place of residence at the time of his first submission to the project.